An Autobiography of a CHRISTIAN HERETIC

JIM ROSEMERGY

Printed in the United States of America.

Library of Congress Control Number: 2022944690

ISBN	Paperback	978-1-68536-785-5
	eBook	978-1-68536-890-6

Westwood Books Publishing LLC
Atlanta Financial Center
3343 Peachtree Rd NE Ste 145-725
Atlanta, GA 30326

www.westwoodbookspublishing.com

Preface

There are some who say there is no such thing as a Christian heretic. If you are a heretic, you cannot be a Christian because your beliefs are false. They are heresy, for they do not conform to the church's dogma, but what if the so-called heretical beliefs are actually true. What if they are what Jesus and Paul actually taught?

Isn't it interesting that we respect and acknowledge the achievements and insights of ancient explorers of science and medicine, but we do not cling to their "truths" when new discoveries open new possibilities? We do not consider new scientific or medical breakthroughs heretical. We no longer bleed disease from our bodies or adhere to classical Newtonian physics when launching a spacecraft to Mars. We honor the past, stand upon the accomplishments of its geniuses, see a little farther, and march toward a more distant horizon. However, when it comes to the greatest quest, the spiritual journey, we often fail to lift our heads to see the receding horizon. The spiritual insights of past saints and theologians are canonized, dogmatized, and offered for memorization and adherence. We are required not to stand on these past insights so we can see a more distant horizon; we are required to stand under them, and their shadow becomes an eclipse that hides the light of new discoveries.

I refuse to stand in the shadow of those who have come before me. I admire their genius, but most of them thought they lived on a flat earth and slavery was acceptable. I accept the label of Christian heretic, but I say I am an explorer of the faith, an explorer of the kingdom of heaven. I accept this mantle although it is the reason some call me a heretic.

An Autobiography of a Christian Heretic tells the tale of how the son of a Coast Guardsman, James Clifford Rosemergy and his wife, Evelyn Dupree O'Neal, an Outer Banker, discovered and followed a path different from the one first encountered as a boy. It is the story of how different interpretations of the teachings of Jesus and His life can lead to atypical conclusions and a unique way of life. For instance, there is a verse of scripture used to drive a wedge between Christians and the members of other religions that is actually a statement honoring other faiths and spiritual paths. This verse seems to say Christianity is the only way to God, but it can also be viewed as an endorsement of other faiths. We will explore these two viewpoints in one of the chapters to follow.

Can you understand why I use the phrase "Christian heretic?" My life and beliefs are rooted in the teachings of Jesus, but I see not only different meanings in His teachings from thousands of years of established canon; I see the possibility of a different world. These contrary beliefs or interpretations of Jesus' life and teachings are called heretical, and so a new kind of spiritual seeker is created: a Christian heretic.

I write hoping you will find my discoveries valuable or at least worthy of your exploration. If you are a defender of the faith, read no further, but if you have no faith, disregard the beliefs of mainstream Christianity, or are an explorer of spirituality, read on.

In your secret soul, you may think you are alone in your beliefs, but upon reading *An Autobiography of a Christian Heretic,* you may find you have a friend and companion on your spiritual journey. There is another who thinks like you. Actually, there are legion. You may have abandoned spiritual things because you could not bear the thought of a God who punishes and torments eternally. If this was the fundamental Christian belief you could not bear, you are not alone. The God of eternal damnation may have turned you from religion and transformed you into an atheist. I understand. I had the same choice because I rejected the same God; however, the difference between an atheist and me is simple—I kept searching.

The beginning of any autobiography is a question. Is my life of any value or interest to anyone else? Most of us answer "no," but this is not true. Everyone's life is worthy of being explored and examined and made available so others can better understand the raw material that makes a life. The difficulty is actually seeing the life. Life is not simply events because two people can experience the same traumatic happening and live different lives. Events are not the true building blocks of an individual's life.

I seek to rediscover the raw material out of which my life was born and is lived. If the building blocks of a life are not events, what are they? Perhaps choices determine a person's experience. I suspect this is true, but not the decision to do a certain thing.

The raw material of my life is what I choose to believe about others, the world and myself. The building blocks are attitudes, beliefs, and perceptions, and so we move from things that happened to me to what happened *in* me. This is the clay that becomes a life. Thoughts, attitudes, beliefs, and feelings are the raw stuff out of which my life was born, continues to be born, and grow.

Plato in the *Dialogues* attributed the following statement to Socrates, "The unexamined life is not worth living." Here I am in my 70's, having crossed the median of my earthly life, and I have just now decided to answer the inner urge to explore my being. Perhaps this expedition into my soul will call you to a similar exploration. I hope to meet you on the journey, and I trust the world will be a better place because our interior lives are no longer mysteries to us.

Introduction

Where to begin? Life seems so complex, but it appears to have a single beginning. I drew my first breath on a Sunday afternoon, July 13th, 1947, in a red-brick hospital on the water's edge in Elizabeth City, North Carolina. The doctor attending my mother said he could always tell an Outer Banker (someone who lives on one of the barrier islands of North Carolina) because of their accent. During the hours of labor, my mother cried out over and over again, "Oh my, oh my."

My mother told me that she and my father struggled to have a child. It took months before she conceived. Perhaps I was reluctant to join the human family. Supposedly, this was the beginning, but the exploration of my life uncovered one beginning after another.

I love the statement, "I am a spiritual being having a human experience living in a spiritual universe governed by spiritual law." *An Autobiography of a Christian Heretic* explores this journey. I will not extensively reveal what happened *to* me; I will reveal in detail what happened *in* me and how it influenced my thoughts, beliefs, attitudes, perceptions and behavior. My hope is that as you read, your head will imperceptibly nod up and down, as at first your unconscious self recognizes something in my journey that is also yours.

Part of me wants to tell you I was a farmer, but records say I was a Naval Aviator, a teaching tennis professional and a minister, yet the truth is, I am a farmer, for I cast seeds, not those surrounded by a husk, but seeds of thought and belief and feeling that cracked the husk of my humanity, allowing a divine embryo to emerge. I want to tell you about the fields where the seeds were sown, but my true purpose is to show you the seeds and their harvests, the vast fields of possibilities.

A seed was sown in the office of a psychiatric nurse as I cried while telling her of my desire to donate a kidney to a person in need. On that day, tears fell and so did seeds. I remember the joy that shook my body as I placed my Navy flight jacket in a box and wrapped it to give to my son Jamie as a Christmas gift. Something sprouted in me at Christi Smith's house in Spokane, Washington, as I looked at a rose bush at the end of her driveway and felt "God pass by."

People tore at the husk of my humanity and demanded that I forgive them. I did, but only after I realized I had grown and therefore was a new person, a person who was never harmed by the individual I resented for years. One friend, Thelma Hembroff, opened a new door to my life when she asked that I sit in silence with her each morning before ministerial classes began. Nancy, my beloved wife, sees only the best in me, even when I hide any interior goodness as thoroughly as it can be hidden.

Dr. Winston Peter Riehl introduced me to tennis and through his calm demeanor asked me without saying a word to find peace within me that allowed my best tennis to be played. Ed Davenport, my best friend, taught me about friendship and generosity and helped me see that exploration is the height of human experience, not a journey to a foreign land, but an inner journey into the kingdom of heaven.

People were teachers and sowers of seeds, but so was silence, so was the presence of God whispering in the night, "Your life is a prayer that I am praying." This God-given revelation created years of confusion that finally cleared during an illness in which I wrote *The Prayer That God Prays.* During a time when I was trying to strip away the mystery of life, my God reminded me, "Unless mystery is part of your life, I am not part of your life, for I am mystery."

As I relate these events to you, I see that much of my life was a trail of tears, not often tears of anguish, but proof that something wanted out and was so unknown to me that it could only emerge as tears. Writing these few words resurrects a memory of a time during a prayer service when I was so filled with joy that tears streamed down my cheeks. Because I thought men did not cry, I tried to suppress the tears and burst a blood vessel in my left eye, leaving a grayed blind spot that reminded me feelings are to be loosed in the world, not remain residents of the physical body. See what I mean? An event, a prayer service, evoked tears that contributed to my trail of tears, but there is much more—the realization that life is to be fully experienced not hidden from myself, others, or the world.

Dear friend, *An Autobiography of a Christian Heretic* mines the raw ore of the deep shafts that lead to the depth of my soul, and you will discover as I have that the most valuable gems that shine like the sun were once dark ore considered worthless.

Do you understand? Events, yes, but much more was present. Emotions and thoughts circled one another, creating a whirlwind of life and an updraft of consciousness that lifted me to new heights. Things happened, but at the place and time of a happening, a vortex formed that transcended time and space. Life happened. Life was lived. It is this life I want to share with you, but I do so not so there is a record of my life, but so you will remember the vortex, your own circling thoughts and emotions, and consider that you, too, are a spiritual being having a human experience.

Come, let us go to Mount Horeb.

CHAPTER ONE

The Shepherd and I

What Is Your Name?

I stood in the shadows at the foot of Mount Horeb and watched a shepherd slowly and deliberately take off his shoes while continuing to stare at a burning bush. Setting his sandals aside, the shepherd faced the bush and asked an audacious question, speaking to the voice that commanded he remove his shoes: "What is your name?"

To know the name of another is to know the nature of the one and to command a degree of power over the one foolish enough to reveal his name. To ask such a question of an unseen presence speaking through the flames of a bush on fire and not consumed is a way to determine if the voice is genuine, the voice of God or a demon. This is the dilemma; it is blasphemy to know the name of God. Surely, no genuine god would answer such a question, but I heard the reply gliding down the slope of the mountain filling me and the valleys of the earth, "I am that I am." In that moment a tradition shattered, for Moses and I knew this was the voice of the Creator revealing not only Its name, but, also Its nature—pure Being.

I never forgot Moses' question and Elohim's reply, but the answer given on Mount Horeb created more questions. Like Moses,

I asked my God again and again, "What is your name, what is your nature, what are you like?" But I added my own query, "why is your name and my first realization of being, *I am*, so similar?" For years answers poured upon me not from a burning bush or in the sound of a mighty wind, but as a voice still and small.

This book is what I heard, but please know that hearing is not knowing. Answers and insights came, but they had to be understood. Often this took years. The voice spoke, and it is still speaking, but it shares only what I can bear.

What was given took me on a journey beyond god, a journey beyond the god of tradition, the god of the past, the god of dogma, and the god of the church.

Half Way There

One particular discovery gave me solace one moment and took it away a moment later. One night I prayed and meditated, and a thought came to me, "You are half-way there." Immediately, I thought, one more step and I am homeward bound, blessed as few are blessed. And then another thought quickly followed, "And you always will be."

I am half-way there, and I always will be. From hubris to humbling in just a few moments. It took months before I understood the gift given that night. I am always half-way there because the journey is infinite. There is no end; just another beginning. The true god of today will be the false god of tomorrow. Today's truth will be tomorrow's error.

This gift, *I am half-way there and I always will be*, is a provision of an explorer. Because of this gift, I was willing to put aside helpful "truths" that burned away the mist of the mountain and brought me to new vistas of understanding, so I could see another trailhead to the summit.

I also learned that the trailhead to new understanding often was marked by absurd assertions. One Sunday morning I was strolling in the community rose garden adjoining the Raleigh Little Theater where the pioneer ministry I served, Unity of Raleigh, held it services. I sat on a bench surrounded by towering oak trees. I looked up and saw the uppermost branches of the trees swaying in the wind. I thought there was a strong wind above that I could not feel on the bench where I sat, but then a strange thought, an absurd thought, came to me, "The wind isn't moving the branches of the trees, the trees are moving and creating the wind."

"Weird," I thought. "Trees don't move and create the wind."

I never forgot the experience and its message. I concluded that it is important to be able to consider strange, weird, and absurd thoughts when exploring spirituality and the mysteries of God. If everything had to satisfy my logical mind, I wouldn't get far on this journey into the greatest mysteries of the cosmos. Some new insights caused my soul to jump for joy, others plunged me into confusion. I must admit there was at first more confusion than joy.

So, let us open ourselves to new understanding and the telling of strange things, but remember, the only insights given are those we can bear, are those we are capable of receiving and comprehending. In some mysterious way, *An Autobiography of a Christian Heretic* found its way into your hands. I conclude, therefore, that you can bear what is written; you can understand it and apply the ideas to your daily life.

And so, come with me. Let me show you my journey. If you are like me, there will be confusion, but do not be concerned, for I have learned, and you will learn, that confusion is the mother of wisdom.

These are our first provisions for this expedition into the unknown.

1. We are always half-way there.
2. The true god of today will be the false god of tomorrow.
3. It is vital to be willing to entertain absurd thoughts.
4. The only insights given are those we can bear.

Come, let us return to Mt. Horeb.

CHAPTER TWO

The First Evidence

Pure Consciousness

It was appropriate that our journey began on Mount Horeb, for all spiritual paths include times of aloneness. As we see the mountain in the distance, we give allegiance to the meaning of its name—solitude. The wind may whisper as it stirs the leaves of the trees or roars in mountain passes, but as we approach the slopes of Mt. Horeb, we become more quiet, more reflective and contemplative. Like Moses on the slopes of the mountain, we tend the flocks of our mind. We camp and the stars ignite in the night sky. So bright is their light that we can feel their weight, but there is another fire we see in the distance. Its mystery calls us and as we draw near, we see a bush on fire, yet not consumed. We know we are on holy ground. We remove our shoes and ask the name, the nature, of the God of fire and light, and the answer comes, "I am that I am. I am pure being. I am the First Light, the light of the awakened cosmos."

It is interesting and noteworthy that such an encounter was the beginning of one of the longest enduring faiths of human spirituality, Judaism, but it is also the beginning of the journey beyond the god of religion and ritual, the god of the church and its dogma, for the God revealed is not a being, but pure being, pure consciousness.

Mt. Horeb and this experience beckon to every seeker. Even the ancient ones, our ancestors who were barely human, felt the call and sensed the light of the bush ablaze. Their path, the spiritual path of humanity, was sinuous, but with every step, humanity moved closer to Mt. Horeb and the discovery of God beyond the god of form. When humanity's spiritual journey began, there was no burning bush and declaration, "*I am that I am*;" there were only the forces of nature, forces that impacted and influenced our lives.

There are many powerful expressions of nature, and therefore there were many gods. Earth, wind, water, and fire were elevated to the height of divinity. Humanity also bowed to the mystery of the sun, moon, and stars. Imagine the wonder of the night sky devoid of light pollution and the smog of modernity. Once we transitioned from hunter-gatherers to farmers, the moon and its phases and the sun and stars' systematic journey across the sky guided our efforts to grow our crops.

Living near the mountains and experiencing the mist, fog, storms, lightning, and the rumbling of thunder magnified reverence and fear of the Creator. Perhaps fear first motivated our worship as we assumed the gods wanted something from us. For thousands of years, sacrifice was the primary form of worship, culminating with the belief that Jesus who gathered to Himself the sins of the world was sacrificed to appease the God He called Father. We believed the only way to salvation or the maintenance of order in our world was sacrifice. This was our assumption. And we were wrong.

We did not understand the gods, but we began to understand ourselves. How natural it was to make God in our image. We were angry, and therefore God was angry, too, and the Creator's rage outweighed our own, threatening to destroy us and creation. Myths of flood, fire, pestilence, and plagues abound in our holy writ—the justice and retribution of an angry God displeased with its creation.

Observation of our outer world dominated our lives and shaped our understanding of the mystery in which we lived. The amazing thing is that we did not simply observe the outer world, we wondered about its origin and the unseen forces that shaped it.

Wondering

Wondering was the first evidence of a spiritual journey, the Creator's first movement in Its creation. Wonder was our first hint that the Creator dwelt in us. Grand questions were asked about creation, our origin and death. Primitive answers were given, beliefs formed, myths were passed from generation to generation, but there was nothing primitive about our wondering.

Our first wonderings gave birth to the question, what is God? The answers were obvious: earth, wind, water, fire, sun, moon, stars, etc. Eventually, naturally, another question arose, who is God?

We took a leap in awareness. Behind the simple question, who is God, is the idea that God could take a form other than the forces of nature and heavenly bodies. The Creator could assume human form. God could be individualized as a human being. What tribal leader or king took this momentous leap in human potential, we do not know, but we know it happened, for a leader assumed the power and authority of a god on earth.

The evidence of an evolving understanding of the divine is undeniable. We have moved from a distant God of the mountain, El Shaddai, fierce as lightning and a raging storm and as mysterious as fog and mist on its slopes, to a distant god burning bright in the sky touching us with warmth that we feel on our faces.

The myth of the Tower of Babel revealed our attempt to reach for a distant God, but then a leap occurred. Why not build a home for God to dwell among us, a tabernacle when we wandered and a temple when we found our home in a promised land? And yet, God was still distant. Living alone in a cube-shaped room, visited once a year by a high priest.

Temple after temple was built, and God became a God of the people, nearby, yet distant and just as fierce as ever. And then another leap occurred; what if God not only dwelt among us, but within us, closer than hands and feet; closer than breathing—an inner light, a life force that animated us and made our bodies a temple?

God in the Midst of Us

Jesus asked His followers to rise up in consciousness and entertain the possibility that the God of the Tabernacle lived not just in a desert tent and on the Temple Mount, but in each individual; that each body was a temple of the living God.

Perhaps when Jesus learned the history of His people and their 40 years of wandering in the wilderness and the construction of the Tabernacle, He saw this vision during His time alone in the desert. A Hebrew rising in the morning pushes aside the flap of his tent, bends so he can exit his desert dwelling and stretches as he looks to the center of the encampment of recently freed Egyptian slaves. He and his tribe are in their assigned positions according to one of the cardinal points of the compass. His eyes focus on the Tabernacle in the midst of the twelve tribes of Israel.

Wonder and joy fill the newly freed slave, for he gazes at the place of the kingdom of God. In the Holy of Holies in the Tabernacle dwells his God, the Nameless One that projects a column of fire at night and a pillar of smoke by day. What a gift—the Creator dwells among them in the center of their encampment and travels with them in the Ark of the Covenant!

Perhaps Jesus saw this vision and expanded upon it when He declared that the kingdom of God, the kingdom of heaven, is in the midst of us—not as the axis mundi, the center of the world, in a host of tents, but in the center of each of us, closer than hands and feet; closer than breathing.

When Ben, our second son, was old enough to ponder spiritual things, I talked with him about his favorite stuffed animal, Pop, a polar bear, turned gray by hugs and child's play. It was obvious when Ben hugged his bear that he felt love. I asked Ben, "Where does the love come from when you hug, Pop?" He said the love came from his stuffed animal.

I challenged Ben by telling him that Pop was filled with stuffing, not love, and that the love Ben felt came from within him. The love was inside of Ben, and when he hugged his bear, he felt it. (I wonder whether I, an eager father wanting his son to understand spiritual things, should have posed this question to Ben at such a young age, but I can assure you that to this day Ben remembers the interaction, and that now as an adult he is aware of the love that is within him and all people.)

The discovery that God dwells within us is an important insight on the journey beyond the god of tradition and the dogma of religion. It causes us to turn within and to wonder about our capabilities and how our potential can be expressed. We wonder, if we are so powerful, why do we feel weak and powerless at times. We wonder about the vastness of the kingdom that dwells in us and how we can explore it, and what are the conditions to be met before the love and power within can find their way into our lives and the world.

Our Desires

Remember, wondering is the first evidence that God exists. The second sign that God exists is our desires. The word "desire" means *of the father, from above*, or *from the stars*, and is testimony that God is seeking expression in and through and as us. If we trace a desire to its origin within us, we will find it is wholesome and divine. Desires are God whispering in our inner ear. "I am in you; I am the essence of your being seeking expression in your life and in the world."

Remember these two words—wonder and desire. They were the first movement of the divine in us, and they are just as active today as they were in the first humanoid to realize "I am."

Indeed, the journey to Mt. Horeb, the journey beyond the god of form and religion is a sinuous one. We are always wondering, and God is always moving in us as our wholesome desires. In this quiet, gentle way, our Creator is calling us higher. We wonder about the closeness of God. Is God in us like a child is in a mother's womb, or a pit in a peach, or like the ocean is in a wave or like an oak tree is in an acorn? How close is the Divine? Was there a god of earth, wind, water, fire, sun, moon, and stars? Was there a god of vegetation that lived for a season and died only to return in the spring when the sun returned to a particular intersection of sky and earth? Was God always within us, more than in the center of an encampment of wandering Hebrews? What other life could there be to cause our breath and wondering? Who or what is the God that fills us with desires?

Now our wondering causes us to consider the God revealed on Mount Horeb, the deity Moses heard say, "*I am that I am*." This is where we are. This is where I am, on the slopes of Mount Horeb, struck with the thought that when I was born, my first realization, the first name I spoke was not "mama or dada," but the name of God—I am.

More provisions for the journey….

1. All spiritual paths lead to Mt. Horeb.
2. Wondering is the first evidence of a spiritual journey, the first hint that the Creator exists and dwells in us. The second sign is desire. All desire can be traced back to the Creator's purpose of expression in and through and as us.
3. Our first realization of being is pure consciousness echoing the revelation of God's name and nature given to Moses on Mt. Horeb—I am.

Come, let us witness the moment of our creation.

CHAPTER THREE

The One Becomes The Many

In The beginning...Possibilities

It is the first day. The First Light shines. It knows It exists. It is pure consciousness. It is awake, conscious; It declares, I Am that I Am. There is no fear, no separation; nor is there a man to till the ground, no Adam, no Eve. There is no good or evil, for there is no garden, there is no forbidden tree or fruit. The tree of the knowledge of good and evil is not even a seedling. There is wondering, curiosity, a yearning to know the depths of Itself, to become more aware, and there is an innate and natural desire to create, to express. Pure consciousness, God, is pure being, but it is also infinite possibilities yearning, desiring to come into manifestation.

There is only one way for creation to proceed. The First Light must give birth to infinite points of light. This moment is recorded in scripture as an echo of the original creation story. It is the first manifestation of the consciousness God is.

> *In the beginning was the Word, and the Word was with God, and the Word was God. He was in the beginning with God. All things were made through Him and without Him nothing was made that was made.*
>
> John 1:1-3

These three verses of scripture describe the next step in the creative process—the One becoming the many. It is the creation of the principle of individuality. This principle is the foundation of our being and the universe we are exploring. Without the principle of One becoming many, we would not exist, and there would be no physical universe.

Individuality was the First Light's creation. It was Consciousness' first creative act after awakening to Its own being.

The First Creative Act

Before exploring the implications of the first three verses of the gospel of John, let us explore the principle of the One becoming the many, the First Light becoming many points of light.

All sports are expressions of the principle of individuality, the one becoming the many. Football, for instance, has a book of rules that outline how the game is played. During football season, on Friday nights, in thousands of cities and towns, the rules of football are individualized as thousands of high school teams compete against one another. The rules seem rather dull, but the games are not. They are filled with possibilities, with twists and turns, with comebacks and triumphs and defeats. The games are individualized expressions of the rules of football.

On Saturday, college teams take to the fields, and on Sunday professional teams play against one another. Year after year, the rules are displayed for our enjoyment. The games are individualized expressions of the rules that are on display as football games played on Friday, Saturday, and Sunday.

A recipe is another example of individuality, the one becoming the many. How many times can a single recipe be cooked, baked, or "expressed?" Grandma's apple pie is an individualized expression of her apple pie recipe. The recipe's possible expressions are many, infinite. Generation after generation of young and old delight in the individualized expression of grandma's special mixture of apples, flour, shortening, sugar and spices.

Remember when you learned the characteristics of a triangle? A three-sided, two-dimensional geometric form whose three interior angles total 180 degrees. How many triangles could you draw? The answer: many, an infinite number. How many different shapes and sizes of triangles were possible? Again, the answer is many, an infinite number. From the one principle of what a triangle is, many triangles are possible.

The wonder of wonders is that each of us is an expression of the One, the First Light, the pure consciousness that God is. We are made in the image and after the likeness of the First Light, for we are the light of the world. We are not stars burning in the heavens; we are points of light shining on earth. We are made in the image and after the likeness of the pure consciousness of the Creator, for we, too, are conscious and driven by an innate desire to wonder, to create and to express.

The First Light Speaks

Now let us return to the implications of the Apostle John's insight into the creative process. I can imagine the Apostle John on the slopes of Mt. Horeb, resting in solitude, as the First Light shines in him and silence speaks.

> *...He was in the beginning with God. All things were made through Him, and without Him nothing was made that was made.*
>
> John 1:2-3

Who is "He?" It is not Jesus. Jesus comes later, when the Word becomes flesh (John 1:14). "He" is the First Light individualized, the image and likeness of pure consciousness, a divine pattern or blueprint guiding the expression of the infinite lights that will shine throughout the cosmos.

Jesus was aware that He was an individualized expression of the First Light He called Father. He declared it when He said, "He who has seen Me has seen the Father" (John 14:9).

The Invisible Man

On August 13, 1976, I was ordained a Unity minister. It was time to get to work, to find a congregation to serve. In Unity, ministers in search of employment "try out" at a church. We arrive at a ministry for a long, active weekend. The agenda usually includes teaching a class, conducting a prayer service, meets-and-greets, interviews and, of course, a Sunday service including a talk and prayer/meditation time with the congregation.

Several months before the tryout, each of us in ministerial training was required to create and present our "tryout" talk to our fellow students. My lesson was entitled, "The Invisible Man," and it was based on Jesus' statement, "He who has seen Me has seen the Father" (John 14:9). Essentially, the lesson stressed that each of us is an individualized expression of the One, that our destiny is to be a place where God appears on earth, that ideally when we speak Truth is heard and love, peace, and joy are felt. As human beings, we become invisible men and women; we become transparent, and what shines forth is the First Light, the pure consciousness God is.

The idea of the invisible man must have resonated with the 18 people of the study group in Raleigh, NC because they hired me as their minister. We first met in the Mission Valley Inn in a basement meeting room, and we explored the heretical teaching that each of us is the light of the world and is destined to be a place where the First Light shines.

Nancy and I were at Unity Church of Raleigh for seven years, and we cherished our time with the people as we moved from the Mission Valley Inn to the Raleigh Little Theater to the purchase of a church building on Glenwood Avenue. In seven years, we grew from 18 spiritual pioneers to more than 300 seekers. Day by day, I witnessed the transparency that Jesus said was available to us. I never thought of it until this moment, but it was a ministry of invisible men, women, and children letting the First Light shine.

It is revealing that Jesus said He was the light of the world, He was an expression of the First Light, but He also proclaimed that we are the light of the world and that we are to let the Light shine, so that those who see it give glory to God. In other words, the consciousness we express is to shine forth in a way that it is evidence not of a human being, but of a cosmic consciousness active on earth.

The First Light individualized has many names. In its primitive form, it is the idea of the perfect being central to many religions. For Christians, this is Jesus; for a Buddhist, it is Buddha; for Hindus, individuality bears the name Krishna; and Islam yearns for its perfect one— the Hidden Imam. The "He" John writes about is the principle through which all will be made manifest. It is the blueprint of the Master Builder. In truth, we are integral to the creative process that is ongoing. We are expressions of the consciousness that God is, the First Light.

A few verses later, John recorded the natural outcome of this creative process, "And the Word became flesh" (John 1:14). This is the First Light or Cosmic Consciousness individualized, expressed, and made manifest. The One becoming the many. The possibilities are infinite. You, dear friend, are one of those possibilities.

And creation continues. "All things were made through Him, and without Him nothing was made that was made; all things were made and are being made through the individualized First Light, the Cosmic Consciousness. This is mind-stretching, (some call it heresy) but wouldn't you expect the discovery of the creative process to expand our consciousness? Remember, consciousness is not static. It is not complete. The First Light wonders and yearns to become more aware. It makes the individualized expressions of consciousness explorers who are always half-way there. There is no contentment until each of us assumes this mantle and accepts our creative role in the universe. It is our responsibility.

We are told that God is changeless, but if God is the First Light, pure consciousness, God is not changeless; God is forever becoming more aware, more conscious, for this quest is central to consciousness. However, principles such as individuality or the speed of light are constant, changeless. (At least until there is a new revelation of an even more fundamental truth upon which the universe is founded. When this happens, the truth of today becomes the error of tomorrow). Nor is God omniscient, all knowing, for there is always more to know. God, the First Light, is ever expanding and becoming more aware and consciousness.

Oneness

In God, in the First Light, there is no fear, no separation. All that is known is one with the One who knows it.

The room was stark, three cushioned metal chairs and a metallic institutional desk facing a wall, ideal for an interrogation. The psychiatric nurse glanced at the paperwork I gave her and pushed away from the desk to face me and my wife, Nancy. The nurse smiled and began the interview. It became an interrogation when she asked if I was promised monetary compensation for the kidney I was willing to donate.

"No," I answered.

"Have you been offered any incentive to donate your kidney," she asked.

"No," I said, "None."

She continued, "Why are you willing to donate your kidney to another person?"

I explained that I knew Carl, that he was a good man serving humanity and that he had many years of service ahead of him. He should be able to serve without limitation, to be able to serve with energy and vitality.

Eventually, the interview/interrogation ended as the nurse praised me for what I was doing. This was when I began to cry. Praise and kind words for what was to come filled me with emotion that I could not contain, emotion that I tried to contain in the past, but now, I let go and let the tears flow.

I told the nurse that the tears were not tears of fear, pain, concern, or anguish, but of joy, that I had been feeling incredible joy at the prospect of donating one of my kidneys to help another person. It was an exuberance that left me giddy, feelings that had me, according to Nancy, bouncing around the house. However, now the joy was taking a new form—tears.

The nurse nodded. She understood. Perhaps she had seen liquid joy before.

The email had come a few weeks before informing hundreds of people of Carl's need. His kidneys were failing, and he needed a kidney transplant or soon he would be on dialysis. Typically, the search for an organ donation takes months if not years. Both Nancy and I expressed our willingness to donate a kidney. Inquiries were made of both of us and several other people who expressed a willingness to donate, but I was picked for advanced testing. I told the person who called that my blood type was "O" positive, making me a universal donor.

Blood was drawn and tested, as well as urine. The follow-up phone call was shocking. The nurse said that all was well and looked promising, but that my blood type was not "O" positive.

"What? How can that be? 'O' positive was on my Navy dog tags."

"'O'-positive may have been on your tags, but your blood type is "A positive," the same as Carl's. And in fact, you have two antigens in common."

I had no idea what an antigen was or how helpful it would be for the operation and in dealing with organ rejection. "Wow," I said. "That's great."

The time of dialysis was nearing for Carl. The possibility of the donation moved quickly. Nancy and I drove from our home in Lake of the Ozarks to St. Luke's Hospital in Kansas City, MO, for final evaluation and testing. In the meantime, an interesting process began for Carl and me.

I began to talk to my kidney. The idea for the conversation came from Myrtle Fillmore, a co-founder of the Unity Movement, my spiritual affiliation. In the late 19th century, Mrs. Fillmore was diagnosed with tuberculosis. She was given only a few months to live. Myrtle and her husband, Charles, went on a spiritual quest seeking healing. They attended a lecture by Dr. E. B. Weeks who made an interesting assertion during his presentation. "I am a child of God; therefore I do not inherit sickness." This statement struck Myrtle and her identity began to shift. She wasn't solely the child of earthly parents; she was a child of God, and as a child of God her inheritance from God was not sickness. This expanding revelation led to a spiritual practice that changed my life.

Myrtle realized she had been thinking of herself as weak and sickly. Her premise was that the cells of her body were intelligent and that she was an intelligent woman—she and her cells should be able to communicate. Her first step was to apologize to the cells of her body for thinking of them as weak and sickly. Next, she praised the cells of her body as expressions of divine life and vitality. The result was a healing.

As a Unity student, I heard the story of Myrtle Fillmore's healing many times, and I shared her premise. I am an intelligent being, and there is intelligence innate to the kidney and what it does in the body; therefore, we should be able to communicate.

I mentally told the kidney that it would be leaving my body to go to another person who was in need. That I would be okay because I had another kidney, but that the kidney to be removed would have a new home with an appreciative person. Not only did I prepare the kidney for what was to happen to it; I prepared my body for the trauma it would soon experience.

When Carl and I met the day before the operations, we talked about what each of us was doing. He, too, was involved in "body communication" for the same reason—there is intelligence that operates at numerous levels in our bodies and minds. As I prepared my body and kidney for its departure, Carl was making a home for the kidney he would receive. This resulted in an amazing and astounding happening that surprised the doctors and nurses.

On the day of the procedures, I went first. Carl and his partner Steve visited with Nancy while my operation began, and as it progressed, Carl eventually left to prepare to receive the kidney, an operation that would take hours. Typically, when a new kidney is sewn into place in its new body, it takes hours, perhaps a day or more, before it begins to function. Amazingly, when my kidney was inserted into its new home and became Carl's kidney, it functioned immediately. Apparently, it is helpful for an organ to know in advance when it will be taken from its long-time home and provided with a new one!

Interestingly, the two operations took place in different hospitals because of the preferences of the two primary surgeons. A day later l was transported by what seemed like two bronco riders in a medical transport van to St. Luke's hospital to be near Carl. It seemed to me that the driver of the van hit every pothole between the hospitals. Not fun.

Carl and I were in a corridor by ourselves and across the room from one another. I could hear his agony in the night as he recovered from the operation that was much more involved than mine.

A day after the operation, I received my "compensation" for the donation—a dream, a dream I will never forget, a dream that changed what I believe about myself and my fellow human beings. In the dream…

I floated horizontally, about a foot off the ground. Before me was an upright whirlpool of light. Slowly, I moved horizontally through the vibrating vortex of light and emerged in a world like none I had ever seen before. I looked at my arms and hands. They were a translucent blue-white light I could see through. I looked around me. Everything was alive, shimmering with color and life. The hues were more vibrate than anything I had ever seen. Everything was alive, even the land and rocks. Then a voice said, "Love makes all this possible." And the dream ended.

I suspect I saw things the way they truly are, vibrant and alive, in fact, shimmering with light and life. Our bodies are not simply flesh, unless we understand that flesh in its fundamental state is light and life.

This vision did not shock me. Years of living prior to the night of the dream prepared me for the experience. In fact, my life's journey was filled with spiritual experiences. I accepted the voice and its message, "Love makes all this possible."

I believe this is the knowing of pure consciousness, God. Everything is alive and all is one. It is the First Light shining as a human being and all creation.

Much of this book explores the mystery of revelation as the First Light shines in and through and as Its first act of creation—an individualized expression of Itself—the light of the world.

The revelation of the circle of light and the connected, vibrant world of shimmering color is actually the way it is. All that we are conscious of is a part of us. What we know, we know only through our consciousness. We may observe a bird, a sunset, or a distant mountain range, but the observation, the knowing, is in our consciousness. We may feel the grit of sand or smell the fragrance of a spice, but the sensations are a part of our consciousness, the individualized consciousness of the One. The sensations or experiences are not separate from us. If we are conscious of it, it is a part of our consciousness; it is one with us.

The question is, what effect does it have on us? A rock may seem separate from us, but if we are aware of it, it is not separate from us. The rock is now a part of us. If we are hiking in a forest and the rock blocks our path, it affects us differently than if it is a pebble beside the path. If it shimmers like gold, the effect may be different than if it is an ordinary stone. What is important is that we know that all we are conscious of is a part of us, regardless of its effect upon us or our world.

Remember, the First Light, God, wonders and yearns to be more aware. It desires to know Itself, to create and to express. It evolves because it is becoming increasingly aware. This happens on a cosmic level, and it happens in us.

Imagine the awareness that is available to us. One of the doors leading to increasing consciousness is the realization that all we know is a part of us. No thing and no one are separate from us. As the dream after the kidney donation revealed, all is connected.

More provisions for the journey…

1. All things were made through Him, and without Him nothing was made that was made. The "Him" is the First Light individualized.
2. We, the many, are individualized expressions of the One.
3. A fundamental law of creation is: The One becomes the many.
4. What we know, we know through our consciousness.
5. All that we are conscious of is a part of us. It may appear separate from us, but it is not.

We have witnessed the moment of our creation. Now let us discover why we were born.

CHAPTER FOUR

The Light of the World

Womb of Creation

Creation began not as a big bang, nor waves of electromagnetic radiation expanding from a centerless universe at the speed of 186,000 miles per second, but with light, with Consciousness. Consciousness is the First Light, the mysterious God of being whose name is: *I am that I am*. This was and is the center of creation. If there was a big bang, this was its womb.

Jesus knew He was an expression of the First Light. It dawned in him that He was not the only expression of the First Light; He was one of many points of light, many individualized expressions of Consciousness. He also understood the natural yearning of Consciousness to become increasingly aware and to express. The First Light must shine, it is the nature of light, but when it walks the earth it has a new name—"the light of the world." Jesus said, "I am the light of the world," (John 8:12) but He also called for His fellow points of light to shine:

> *You are the light of the world. A city that is set on a hill cannot be hidden...Let your light so shine before men that they may see your good works and glorify your Father in heaven.* (Let your consciousness express in such a way that others will know it is not you, but the Father, the First Light, that is expressing.)
>
> Matthew 5:14, 16

The Jesus Experience

When I was in ministerial school in the mid 1970's, I took a class, Fillmore Fundamentals, in which we studied the beliefs of Charles Fillmore, co-founder of the Unity Movement. The students were divided into panels or groups of three who were to investigate Charles Fillmore's beliefs about a specific subject, and then report their findings to the class. In addition, each student was to tell the class about his or her personal beliefs about the assigned subject. My panel was assigned the subject of Jesus.

Like all the ministerial students, I researched Charles Fillmore's statements about Jesus, but I was less certain about my own beliefs. The night before my panel was to present its findings, I arrived home at 10:45 p.m. after my work as a teaching tennis pro. While preparing for bed I said to Nancy, "I wish Jesus would come to me and tell me what He is all about."

Immediately, I felt a presence, an urging from within. I went alone into the living room of our mobile home and sat quietly with a legal pad and pen and recorded what I saw and heard. *Jesus was standing on a mountain top and looking at humanity. He said, "You can do the things that I do." Then he looked away from us toward higher mountain peaks in the distance. He then looked back at us and added, "and greater things than these shall you do."* (The quotes attributed to Jesus are found in John 14:12.)

The next morning Nancy told me that while she was reading her novel before falling asleep, a verse of scripture kept filling her mind again and again. I asked what scripture. She said, *"You can do the things that I do and greater things then these shall you do."* I was amazed that although Nancy did not experience the vision, the consciousness of Jesus was so strong in our home that she felt the essence of my Jesus experience.

I believe Jesus visited me that evening in answer to my plea to understand His mission. It is interesting as a side note that during my oral exams before being approved for ordination as a Unity minister, one of my examiners was interested in this experience. (He must have been told of the event by a member of the faculty.) He asked me, "What is the difference between you and Jesus?" A one-word answer came to mind, "Consciousness." This reply satisfied the minister on my Licensing and Ordination Committee.

After this oral examination, the minister who asked me what the difference was between myself and Jesus followed me out of the room. He told me that while he was flying to Unity Village to do his work on the Licensing and Ordination Committee, he sat next to a man, and they started talking. The man said he was coming to Kansas City to see his son ordained as a Unity minister. The man was my father. The Licensing and Ordination committee member then told my father that he was on the team that would determine if I would be ordained or not.

The minister then told me how proud my father was of me. What an incredible series of events all beginning with the yearning for Jesus to tell me the reason for His ministry.

This happening that I call the "Jesus experience" reveals the potential of each human being. Jesus stands on a pinnacle of consciousness, and we, too, can stand on this summit of awareness. In the vision, when Jesus looked away from us, He saw higher vistas of awareness for Himself, higher states of consciousness that one day would dawn in each of us—that is why Jesus said, *"...and greater things than these shall you do."*

This is consistent with the provision for the journey—we are always halfway there, and it reinforces the idea of the ever-expanding consciousness of God.

Jesus is our Way-Shower blazing a trail of consciousness for us to follow, calling us to let our light shine, but we tend to discount our potential as expressions of the First Light and lights of the world.

The Oak and the Acorn

An acorn lay on the ground and looked up at a majestic oak tree towering over it. The acorn said, "O mighty oak tree, I will build an altar to you and worship you."

The oak tree lowered its branches slightly and said to the acorn, "You can do the things that I do and greater things than these shall you do."

"Oh, no," replied the acorn. "Look at you. I am nothing like you. You reach for the sky; I lie on the ground. Oh, no, we are not alike. You are a god tree reaching for the heavens, I am an acorn, born of the grit of the ground."

"You know not the truth of your own being," answered the oak tree. "You were born high in my branches. I am what you are and what you are destined to be. Within you is the potential to reach for the sky. You can do the things that I do and greater things than these shall you do."

This vignette illustrates humanity's typical relationship with Jesus. We fail to understand the universal principle of individuality and that although Jesus was an amazing expression of God, the First Light, His purpose was to reveal to us the nature of the Consciousness we are all destined to discover and express. It is why He acknowledged that He was the light of the world, and that we, also, are the light of the world, commissioned not only to reach for the light, but to let the light, the ever-expanding First Light, shine from within us and as us.

Further evidence of our divine potential is Jesus' commandment that we love one another as He loved us. It is unlikely that Jesus would command us to love as He loved unless it was possible. He could have commanded us to love one another, a reasonable request, but He challenged us to fulfill our potential and to love one another as He loved us. Loving as Jesus loved seems unlikely if not impossible, just as unlikely as it is to imagine an acorn becoming a mighty oak tree.

Stan and I and Mississippi Mud

There are immense possibilities within us. I first experienced this potential as strength when I was a teenager. Stan was younger than I, but much taller. He would attend college and play basketball. We were playing at a housing construction site. Numerous homes were in various stages of completion.

Pits were dug and because the neighborhood was below the top of the levees and the nearby Mississippi River, the pits filled with water. Stan slid down the edge of one of the pits and toppled into the dark, muddy waters. I laughed as he clawed at the side of the hole, but then he went under and came up gasping for air. Stan was in trouble. He panicked. The slick Mississippi mud prevented him from getting a hand-hold to pull himself from the water.

I slowly slid down the side of the pit and perched on the water's edge, digging into the mud to prevent me from joining Stan in the water. I reached out and grabbed Stan under his arms and with my arms fully extended lifted his body out of the water and pulled him over me. We crawled to safety.

The strength to pull Stan from the water was more than physical. It was divine. Imagine raising a dripping wet boy larger than yourself vertically out of a pit while perched on the slick side of a hole covered in Mississippi mud. There is no way I possessed such strength, but such strength was available. We do not possess it, but it is available to us, it can flow through us when we forget ourselves and serve the needs of another.

Trouble Ahead?

Creation continues as the Cosmic Consciousness, the First Light, expands and grows in awareness. Points of light spread across the universe, but there are complications. Once we stood before a burning bush not consumed, but now a seedling is growing and soon it will mature and present to the individualized expressions of the First Light a choice. Will we eat of the Tree of the Knowledge of Good and Evil or will we not?

More provisions for the journey….

1. We are the light of the world.
2. We are individualized expressions of the First Light, the pure consciousness that God is.
3. The lights of the world have a choice.

Come, be not afraid; it is time for us to stand before the Tree of the Knowledge of Good and Evil.

CHAPTER FIVE

When Light Is Night

The First Light is to shine in and through and as us, so others may know the light, follow the light and become bearers of the light, but our light can be darkness.
Jim Rosemergy

Trouble in Paradise

The universe is expanding. God, the First Light, knows It exists, for It perpetually sings Its song, "*I am that I am.*" It is curious. It wonders. Driven by the desire to know more, to become increasingly aware of what it is to be, the First Light shines as many points of light. Each light, each consciousness, is an individualized expression of God. Each point of light is conscious and perpetually declaring, "I am."

We are these points of light, each an integral part of the ongoing creation. Jesus called us the light of the world. We are to shine in a way that when people see our light, witness our consciousness being lived, they know it is not a personal light, but the First Light of long ago shining in the cosmos today. We live not only as expressions of the First Light, but so the cosmic consciousness may grow in awareness of what it is to be and express. This is our reason for being, it is why we exist, but often our purpose is unknown to us or forsaken by us.

The First Light, the pure consciousness God is, is not changeless. It is growing and evolving, but in all Its knowing, It knows nothing of good and evil. Its "eyes" are too pure to know such things. This great truth was declared by the prophet Habakkuk and is recorded in his book in the Bible.

> *You are of purer eyes than to behold evil.*
>
> Habakkuk 1:13

The First Light, the God of pure being, may know nothing of the Tree of the Knowledge of Good and Evil, but for us, the First Light's offspring, the tree is always close at hand. This seedling is growing in our garden, and soon we will stand before it and wonder, "Shall we eat of the fruit of the Tree of the Knowledge of Good and Evil?" We are aware, not only conscious of being, but conscious beings aware of a cosmic choice.

The message is clear: there are states of consciousness where we see, have knowledge of the extremes of life, both good and evil, but there is a state of consciousness where there is no good or evil. We can eat of the Tree of the Knowledge of Good and Evil, or we can adopt the consciousness discovered by Habakkuk and walk past the Tree of the Knowledge of Good and Evil and eat of the Tree of Life.

Two Trees, Two Paths

Jesus walked the sunlit way, but He knew there was another path, sunlit at times and at other times with shadows so deep they were mistaken for night. This path was laid before Him during His temptations. We, too, are called to walk the sunlit way, but there are times when through choice, our consciousness, the light of the world, can be dark and filled with error.

> *If therefore the light that is in you is darkness, how great is that darkness.*
>
> Matthew 6:23

God, the First Light, is consciousness, and we are made in the image of God; therefore, we are consciousness, too. Jesus called God Father, but He called individualized consciousness the light of the world. He called consciousness light because it is through our awareness that we "see," perceive and know ourselves, others, the world and the cosmos. It is a lamp shining in the world that illumines our path, but the light, the consciousness, can be dark.

Our consciousness or knowing can come into being through revelation, the "touch of the First Light," or through living life—better known as trial and error. Jesus recognized that if the light, the consciousness, in us is darkness, how great is that darkness. It is so dark we cannot see; we are blind and do not know the truth. We think we see, for consciousness always knows what it knows, but it may not know the truth. It is convinced that it knows what is true, but it judges by appearances, and therefore walks in darkness. Its world is not real, for it is filled with shadows, illusions, lies and errors. It is a world that has only one inhabitant, the consciousness that sees it.

The eye through which we see is our lamp, for it is through our consciousness that we see our world; however, often, we see dimly, we perceive distorted shapes and know a "truth" that does not exists. We convince ourselves that our perceptions are true, but often they are not. This is what happens when we eat of the Tree of the Knowledge of Good and Evil. Apparently, it is part of the path many points of light, many lights of the world, choose to walk.

I know of no one who has not eaten of the Tree of the Knowledge of Good and Evil. All of us radiate darkness or negativity from time to time. We are unique lamps with the capacity to radiate light and darkness, truth and error. In most instances, light shows the way, but after we have eaten of the Tree of the Knowledge of Good and Evil, our regrets, shame, and guilt point to the path we must now walk. These three shadowy parts of ourselves tell us of the need to return to a state of consciousness without labeling and naming. Regret, shame, and guilt are uncomfortable, but it is this discomfort and discontent that help us return to a path of acceptance, forgiveness and love of self. (More on this when we explore one of the greatest spiritual breakthroughs of my life—the sacred human.)

SERE School

Fear is darkness that can inhabit the soul, and it has its consequences. When I was in the Navy and preparing to go to Vietnam, I received orders to SERE School: Survival, Evasion, Resistance, and Escape. It is prisoner-of-war training. All Navy fliers destined for combat were trained in these skills. My friends who had already attended SERE School were merciless in their descriptions of what was going to happen to me. "Oh, they are looking for someone just like you. They are going to beat the crap out of you. It is going to be misery for days on end."

They painted an image that allowed me to expand the picture and make it even worse for myself. Needless to say, I did not want to go to SERE School, but I had orders.

Suddenly, I was ill with a fever and profound weakness. I was diagnosed with mononucleosis. A friend in high school had the disease, and it took him months to recover. The "good news" was that I could not attend the advanced prisoner-of-war training in my current condition. The plane arrived to take the Navy fliers for the training, and I was not on it. As the plane took off from Naval Air Station, Albany, Georgia, my speedy recovery began. In three days, I was playing tennis again and filled with energy. However, I did not miss the "joys" of SERE School, for I received orders to attend the next class, and it was as miserable as predicted.

As I look back on this experience, I see what fear can do and how it can darken the soul. Rather than face the challenge, I mentally ran from it, and my consciousness produced a way to avoid the trauma, but not for long. I ate of the Tree of the Knowledge of Good and Evil and consequently did not allow myself to discover inner resources that could help me face a traumatic experience as a prisoner of war. Later when I did attend the school, I learned skills I never needed to use because I was not shot down during my 100-plus combat missions; however, I did learn how creative consciousness can be and how debilitating fear can be. I experienced the lamp that was my consciousness "radiating" its darkness. It disrupted the harmony of my physical body as well as my peace of mind.

The Choice

The Tree of the Knowledge of Good and Evil has cast its seeds throughout the cosmos, for each of us must choose whether we will eat the fruit of this tree and come to know good and evil. The tree, the choice, is always so near that we can reach out and pluck its fruit. Even now as we "journey beyond the god of tradition," the tree and its fruit are as near as a thought of condemnation or separation or a feeling of fear or hatred. For us, the lights of the world, the Tree of the Knowledge of Good and Evil will always be in our garden, but it is not inevitable that we eat its fruit. One day, our eyes will be too pure to behold iniquity. This vision will last for only a moment, but it will create a hunger and thirst to see again what the First Light sees. At another time, we will live a day seeing clearly and know that what is seen is the way it really is. Then we will know that the vision is to be more than a moment or a day. It is a vision of a life lived in conscious oneness with all creation.

The good news is that we can become aware of a consciousness in which there is no good or evil, a consciousness in which there is no judgment, no labeling or naming. It is a state of mind and heart in which there are no needs. There is nothing to overcome, nothing to fix and nothing to heal. It is the consciousness of the ever-expanding First Light. This consciousness transforms, strengthens, heals, and guides.

David, the shepherd king and psalmist, was touched by this consciousness when he wrote, "The Lord is my shepherd, I shall not want" (Psalm 23:1). The truth is that when the First Light shines in us, we cannot want. We are content; we are fulfilled. There are no needs. This "no need" state is evidence of the presence of the First Light, and It will manifest itself as our lives. (We will return to the "no need" state later in the book as we explore the depth and intricacies of prayer/meditation.)

We all know the taste of the fruit of the Tree of the Knowledge of Good and Evil. Jesus described those in this state of mind. "… they know not what they do" (Luke 23:34). So true. I know this state of consciousness well.

Let me give you a taste of the Tree of Life in which all are one, there is nothing to overcome, and our eyes are too pure to behold iniquity.

The Way It Is

One evening I was in prayer and meditation, and I caught a glimpse of what it is to be the light of the world, to have the First Light shine through me. These thoughts expanded my being and my world.

I breathe no air, I drink no water, I eat no food. I am the light of the world, pure consciousness. No earthly thing has ever touched me. I have never known cold or hot, for I am pure spirit. No needle has ever penetrated me, no drugs have ever coursed through my being. I am pure light.

I am the mother giving birth and the child being born. I am the farmer sowing seed and the seed that is cast. I am the fruit of the harvest. I am the fishermen fishing and the fish that is caught. I am the wave that is the sea and the droplet of water that falls as rain. I dwell in the mountains and by the sea and in the city. I am every man, woman, and child. I am the light of the world.

Years later while I was preparing the fifth edition and seventh printing of my book, *Living The Mystical Life Today*, a poem came to me. I now see that the poem was written from the same consciousness of that meditative experience that happened many years before.

Who Am I?

Who I am
    Cannot be told.
    The telling is in what I am not.
Who I am
    Does not eat the seed of the earth,
    The fruit of the trees.
    I drink no water.
Who I am
    Doesn't shiver when it's cold
    And grow weary when it's hot.
    I wear no clothes.
Who I am
    Is not pierced by doctor's tools
    Healed by man's elixir.
    I am not sick.
Who I am
    Lacks nothing
    And asks nothing of God.
    For what God can do, God is doing.

Who am I?
I cannot tell.
Only God can answer.
And when I ask, "Who am I?"
God answers, "Who's asking?"

Two Paths Leading To One Path

The laws of creation support the purpose of the First Light—ever-expanding awareness. Wonder and curiosity are the first movements of the God of Being, for the First Light is always being born, always awakening. As "lights of the world," this desire to awaken lives in us. It is our hunger and our thirst. Only the fruit of the Tree of Life can nourish us. This fruit is our living water and our daily bread.

However, when we fail to live by the laws of creation, our consciousness ceases to expand. We are conscious, but not of the truth. What we believe to be true is a lie and does not support the purpose of the First Light—ever-expanding awareness. There is no growth, and we experience the pain of not being true to the purpose of the First Light and our related purpose. There seems to be no light shining. Rather than day, we seem to experience only night, and how great is the night and its darkness.

We have all been in the presence of someone who radiates negativity. Shadows are the absence of light, but they can be seen, and even though they have no being and substance, darkness can etch lines on our face, cause our eyes to fail to shine and dull our speech and depress our spirits. Darkness that has no weight can weigh us down.

We experience a sense of separation from our world and others. Our soul shrivels, our vision is blurred and the horizon stands at our feet. The trap is set, for we have *knowledge* of good and evil. We think we know, that we are wise, and we are convinced that what we see is true, but we are deceived. Our light is night, and we stumble.

Our destiny and purpose are aligned with the curiosity of the First Light—Ever-Expanding Consciousness, but during our journey beyond the god of dogma, we straddle two paths. One is the path of the First Light without good or evil. This path we experience through prayer, meditation, and revelation. The other path is filled with condemnation and judgment, love and hate, anxiety and peace, lack and contentment, hubris and humility, truth and error. It may be that both paths are necessary, but one thing is evident: both paths are trod by nearly all of the "lights of the world."

The reason is the nature of consciousness. It knows what it knows whether what it knows is truth or error. It is convinced until either revelation of the First Light or the pain and limitation of living life informs us that either our light (the consciousness we radiate) is night or that our light (the consciousness we radiate) is day.

More provisions for the journey….

1. We see our world, ourselves, and others through our consciousness.
2. Our consciousness can be rooted in truth or error.
3. The light, the consciousness, we see by and radiate can be dark.
4. The light, the consciousness, we see by and radiate can be an expression of the First Light.

Come let us explore the vast kingdom of consciousness, the consciousness that God is and that we are. Let us live consciously aware of the creative process and how consciousness is like a treasure and a seed, an eye and a lamp, a river, a secret and a veil. It is time to discover the many facets of the jewel that is consciousness and to be humbled by Its power.

CHAPTER SIX

The Crossroads

Repent and Awaken

The word repent means to change one's mind. Jesus began His ministry asking people to change their thinking about the kingdom of God. "Repent, for the kingdom of heaven is at hand" (Matthew 4:17). Most Jews thought the kingdom was established by spiritual forces capable of overthrowing the Roman empire. Jesus asked the people to consider that the kingdom was already here.

A third of Jesus' message to the world was about the kingdom of heaven or the kingdom of God, as it was sometimes called. It is not an earthly realm, but it affects our daily lives and the world. The means through which it is revealed is not violence; it is spiritual awakening and revelation. Notice that Jesus said the kingdom is already here. It is at hand; it is within our grasp. The problem is that we do not see it, that we are unaware of what is present. This is a call to awaken, a call to be conscious.

Jesus spoke of the coming of the kingdom, but what was coming was an awakening, a spiritual breakthrough for the human family, the scales falling from our eyes, so we could see what is present and at hand.

Through more than thirty parables and numerous statements about the kingdom of heaven, Jesus tried to help us see what was and is within our grasp. As we shall see, consciousness is the key.

We may discover the intricacies of mathematics and probe the depths of the atom and witness the dance between matter and energy, but consciousness is the greatest mystery and holds the greatest promise. Consciousness is the creator of all that is; it is the womb where all is born. It is the means through which we probe the cosmos whether we seek the nature of dark matter and dark energy or to know ourselves and the nature of God.

Consciousness is the vessel of exploration, and it is what is explored. We travel far in search of what is close at hand. Like the ancients, we look to the mountain when what we need to know is at our feet, and so if we want to know the nature of consciousness, we must explore ourselves as well as the cosmos where we physically dwell. Both the Creator and the created meet at the crossroads called consciousness. One road is the cosmic consciousness that proclaims, *I am that I am*, the other is a consciousness of ourselves and the cosmos. Obviously, the intersection is awareness, so this is where we begin the next leg of our journey beyond the god of dogma and theology.

Born Anew

Nicodemus, a Jewish religious leader and member of the Sanhedrin, the ruling religious body of Israel, visited Jesus at night because he did not want to be seen talking to Jesus; however, he came in a greater darkness, the darkness of ignorance.

During their time together, Jesus answered an unspoken question that was in Nicodemus' mind and the hearts of the people of Israel, "When will the kingdom of God come?" A natural addendum to this question was another query, "When will we be rid of Rome and its domination of our nation and our lives?"

Jesus' answer to these unasked questions puzzled the religious leader. Jesus said, "...unless one is born again, he cannot see the kingdom of God" (John 3:3). Nicodemus was puzzled, "How can a man be born when he is old? Can he enter a second time into his mother's womb and be born" (John 3:4)? Jesus was astonished that a spiritual leader did not understand that the kingdom "came" to each person through spiritual revelation or birth. "Are you the teacher of Israel, and you do not know these things" (John 3:10)?

Jesus also gave Nicodemus an insight into spiritual birth—that it comes suddenly and without warning. "The wind blows where it wishes, and you hear the sound of it, but cannot tell where it comes from and where it goes. So is everyone who is born of the Spirit" (John 3: 8).

Please know that this birth is not a one-time event. It happens again and again and again. This book is a record of the pangs of spiritual birth I experienced. Revelation, awakening, and birth are the essence of life, and what grows and matures is our consciousness.

Do you remember in a previous chapter I mentioned the need for a spiritual explorer to be willing to entertain absurd thoughts? This attitude is crucial for spiritual breakthrough because often when we encounter a new insight it will at first seem absurd or untrue. At other times the revelation is instantly apparent. What dawns in us does not cloud our vision; it enables us to see...but not always. There are times when we must wrestle with the new insight or at least rest respectfully with it until a flash of light, like lightning, enables us to catch a glimpse of the new landscape where we will live.

Ask For A Question

As I explored the spiritual awakening of several people in the Bible, I saw a pattern in which the awakening was initiated by a question. Usually, in prayer and meditation we ask for answers. One night because of my study of spiritual awakening, I took a new approach. I asked for a question that would stir me, an assertion that would place me before the door of the kingdom of heaven.

This is what happened to Saul who became Paul. He was on the road to Damascus in search of Jesus' followers, so he could arrest them and turn them over to the authorities. In a mystical experience, Jesus posed a question to this persecutor of the early Christians, "Saul, Saul, why are you persecuting Me" (Acts 9:4)? This question shook Saul, flooded him with light that blinded him, shattered his massive ego and forever suspended his quest to arrest Jesus' followers. The revelation of his mental blindness temporarily physically blinded him until a follower of Jesus healed him. Too little light can cause us to stumble, but an abundance of light can also blind us.

Years ago, Nancy and I led a pilgrimage to the Holy Lands. Our guide, Schlomo, took us to the ruins of the steps leading to the Temple Mount. Schlomo invited us to climb the steps. We started our ascent and stumbled again and again. The steps were uneven in height and width. We, pilgrims of modernity, learned the lesson all pilgrims learn when they desire to awaken to God's presence—each step requires focus and conscious attention. The structure of the steps demanded this discovery, but there was another lesson to learn—Saul's realization, that too much light can blind us. The light reflecting off the walls surrounding the Temple complex blinded us. In ancient times, the walk was even more tenuous because the walls were covered with highly reflective stone.

We climbed, stumbling and wiping tears from our eyes. We understood Saul's experience that too much light can blind us. Perhaps Saul recalled his ascent of the Temple steps when light blinded him on the road to Damascus. I will never forget the uneven temple steps and the blinding light as I stumbled again and again on my ascent to the top of the steps.

Simon Peter, one of the original disciples, likewise was awakened by a question. Jesus asked his disciples who were gathered in northern Israel at Caesarea Philippi, "...who do you say that I am"

(Matthew 16:15)? Simon Peter answered, "You are the Christ, the son of the living God" (Matthew 16:16).

Jesus recognized the source of the insight of His faithful disciple. "…for flesh and blood has not revealed this to you, but my Father who is in heaven" (Matthew 16:17). In other words, this insight came from the consciousness of the First Light expressing through Simon Peter. This is revelation; it is spiritual birth, and it is central to a spiritual way of life. It is the way we "see" the kingdom that Jesus insisted is here.

Having seen the power of revelation, I took a new path to spiritual awakening. I stopped asking for answers to my questions and instead asked for questions that would stir me and challenge me. I asked for a question that would break the shell of my humanity and open me to new growth and fruits of Spirit. Asking for a question to stir and challenge me placed my soul in a state of willingness to be provoked, for my world to be shaken and my perspective to be altered. The agent of change was not always a question, but what was received always expanded my consciousness, and magnified my world, so I saw smaller details and perceived subtleties in my life and the world. I behaved differently, more compassionately and lovingly and lived more hours each day in peace committed to being a place where the First Light shined.

During times when I pressed to achieve a goal, I heard, "Nothing needs to happen." When there didn't seem to be enough money, I heard, "It is time to increase your giving." During times of struggle when I considered my life's journey, I heard, "Why do you do what you do?" Sometimes answers and directions were clear and calming, but in most instances, what emerged from within jarred my concept of myself, others and the world. Earthquakes occurred, but things were not falling apart, they were shaking together. This happened so many times that revelations are no longer resisted or ignored. They are added to my list of special friends that shape my world and encourage me to be what I am.

The Nicodemus Society

In many ways, we are a Nicodemus society, ignorant of the dynamics of spiritual awakening. Why? Because humanity's spiritual journey is dominated by ritual, dogma, and a desire to be saved. We do not know that God is consciousness and that this is the image in which we are made. We fail to heed Jesus' call to be born anew, so we can see the kingdom of heaven waiting to be discovered. We look for signs of the coming kingdom and for the appearance of a savior, when Jesus told us all we need to know—that the kingdom is already here, that spiritual birth is required to see it, that we cannot see the birth coming or know where it is taking us. Suddenly, it is upon us, like lightning streaking across the sky, revealing a landscape once obscured by darkness. The fleeting vision touches us and causes us to long to live in the world seen for just a moment. However, now the vision is within us, and Jesus' prophesy is fulfilled, "The kingdom of heaven is within you."

The Kingdom Is A Treasure

This is the way it is with treasure. It is present, but we must have an eye to see and a mind to comprehend. The gold is tumbling in mountain streams waiting for someone to see the glint of light in the water. Diamonds are obscured by dirt and hidden by their innate roughness, waiting for someone to understand their capacity to capture and display the beauty of light.

This is the heart of Jesus' ministry. The treasure, the kingdom of heaven, is here waiting for us to be born anew so we can see the beauty that surrounds us. We must become like children, filled with wonder and curiosity, and in this way, we assume the qualities of the First Light that continues to probe Itself and the cosmos It created.

Return to the Crossroads

We stand in the nexus of the crossroads. In one direction is the physical universe, the depth of the atom, the enormity of stars, planets, nebulae, and black holes. It is certainly worthy of our attention, but although we may explore the physical world, we do so in an unconscious attempt to understand consciousness. We turn in another direction and feel the awe and fear of our ancestors who formed myths about the Creator, and this, too, is an attempt to awaken. We quickly spin to another cardinal point, and we come face to face with ourselves, our bodies, our thoughts and feelings, attitudes and beliefs.

This is where we perpetually stand, in the center of the crossroads of the cosmos, of God and of self. This is where we must be, where the real expedition begins, for the intersection of the cosmos, God, and self is consciousness. All the paths lead back to the center, to the First Light, the lights of the world and their creation. The common ground for the physical universe, God, and self is consciousness. To stand at the intersection of these three is to realize they are not separate from one another. We are not separate from anything. To see this holy trinity, to really see the three is to behold only One, for God is an ever-expanding consciousness, we are individualized expressions of consciousness, we are the One becoming the many, and creation is consciousness made flesh even if that flesh is a star of compressed neurons or a one-cell ameba.

Investigations of the First Light

The One who said *I am that I am* continues to probe Itself and what It creates. It is the Watcher, for it does not label or judge what It sees or knows. The First Light is curious; It wonders. It is pure consciousness that knows nothing of goodness or evil. It chants Its mantra—*I am that I am*—and of all that It knows, It draws a simple conclusion, "It is, and I am aware of it, and because I am aware of it, it is a part of me." In this way, pure being explores and evolves and becomes a cosmic consciousness available to the lights of the world, available to us.

To touch this consciousness, or perhaps it is best to say, to be touched by this awareness, is to enter a no-need state where there is nothing to fix or overcome. There is no naming, no blaming, no labeling, no condemning. There is pure joy, awe, contentment, and knowing. No error or lie is perpetuated. Only truth endures, so there is freedom, freedom to continue to wonder and to explore. This First Light is like a child wanting to touch, taste, and probe all things, wanting to explore the depth of all it knows. It deconstructs matter and finds energy and on closer observation finds Itself. And the wonder of wonder is that all It knows awaits our knowing.

We have access to all that is discovered, and all we discover that is truth expands the consciousness of the First Light. God consciousness gives no credence to shadows, illusions and error, but we who live in human consciousness may believe lies, and therefore put the falsehoods to the test and endure days, months, years, or even lifetimes of pain until we recognize that what we once believed was true is false. The wonder is that cosmic consciousness is available to us, enabling us to avoid the pain of trial and error if we choose the contemplative path of stillness and silence, if our means of discovery is spiritual birth and revelation.

The way we know we have touched the hem of the cosmic cloak is that there is no need to change anything, to fix or repair our lives or the world. There is nothing to overcome, for we are "in the world and not of it." However, this awareness is not the end. It is only the beginning, and although in this state of mind there is no need to change, it is actually the womb that gives birth to our ever-evolving lives and world.

The No Need State

On November 7, 2020, I was in prayer/meditation with Nancy. We made a commitment in March, 2020 to sit in silence for 12 minutes each night until the danger of the Covid-19 pandemic passed. On that November night, I entered the no-need state and experienced the touch of the consciousness of the First Light. These words filled me. "No fear, no lack, nothing to heal, nothing to know, where nothing needs to happen, and where all things are possible."

This is the paradox of creation. We can narrow the possibilities by holding specific outcomes in mind, but this is not the way of the First Light. In God consciousness, there is nothing held in mind; we are at rest, aware. This was David's experience recorded in the 23rd Psalm. "The Lord is my shepherd; I shall not want." No needs, no wants, no lack. Green pastures, still waters. Contentment, joy, peace.

Consider the two ways we can hold something. We can grip a book, for instance, as it is pressed between our fingers and our thumb, or we can let the book rest in the palm of our hands. Both ways of holding the book are part of our journey in consciousness, but the way of the First Light is not a vise, but an open palm. Gripping is an attempt to make something specific happen. An open palm is letting possibilities come into being.

In God consciousness, in the consciousness of the First Light, there is no fear, no separation, no condemnation, no labeling; nothing needs to happen, but this no-need state is an invitation for us to be a place where light shines and creation happens. Interesting isn't it? Nothing needs to happen is an invitation for a new universe to be born, for there to be light.

What Consciousness Can Do

Imagine attending a party where we are unacquainted with the other people in attendance. We don't know them, and they don't know us. Small talk ensues: what is your name? What do you do? Are you married? Do you have children?

Enough of the normal human exchange; it is time to expand the conversation.

I believe everyone must eventually be able to instantly answer two essential questions: What are you, and what is your purpose? And so, we add our far-reaching questions to the mundane queries of the party, and life gets interesting.

"What are you, and why are you here? What is your purpose?"

One day Nancy and I purchased tickets on Southwest Airlines. We stood in line according to our assigned number that determined when we entered the aircraft. A woman seeking to find her place in line looked at me and said, "What are you?"

I know she wanted to know my number, but I replied, "I am a spiritual being." She laughed and laughed. Apparently, knowing who you are is a hoot!

My answers to the two essential questions flow from my spiritual breakthroughs. What am I? I am a spiritual being. I am the child who enters the kingdom of heaven. As a child I wanted to taste everything, so I thrust it into my mouth. I wanted to eat it, to make it a part of me, for if I am aware of something, it is a part of my consciousness, and therefore a part of me.

I am an explorer of the kingdom of God. My purpose is to become increasingly aware. These answers flow from my current understanding of the First Light and the desires implanted in my nature, the same impulses that drive the Creator—wonder and curiosity. Remember, only a child, a wonderer, can enter the kingdom of heaven. This makes me an explorer, and life an adventure, exciting, fresh and new—and challenging.

Sometimes I explore in the day; at other times, I stumble in the night. Sometimes I stand on temple mounts; at other times I enter the darkness of my being. Temple mounts, mountain tops and caves are as different as day and night, but they evoke awe and wonder, fear and joy. So, let us explore the kingdom of God, the intricacies of consciousness and the work that it does.

More provisions for the journey….

1. The kingdom of heaven is at hand; it is within our grasp.
2. The kingdom of heaven is within us.
3. We stand at the nexus of the crossroads.
4. The nexus of the crossroads is consciousness.
5. When we explore the universe, we will always find consciousness, for consciousness is the knower.
6. When we explore God, we will always find consciousness, for consciousness is what knows.
7. When we explore ourselves, we will always find consciousness, for consciousness is the only one who knows.
8. What is known is known to be part of the knower.

Come with me and let us explore the kingdom that is here, the kingdom that is within us. Let us receive the treasure of treasures and marvel at the many facets of the jewel that is consciousness. Let the beauty of the facets of consciousness enable us to better know God, ourselves and the universe.

CHAPTER SEVEN

The Treasure And The Seed

The Pearl of Great Price

Jesus said there was a treasure so valuable that if we found it in a field, we would sell everything in order to purchase the field and possess the treasure. Likewise, He spoke of a merchant seeking beautiful pearls, "who, when he found one pearl of great price, went and sold all that he had and bought it" (Matthew 13:36). Pearls were a great mystery to people of the desert, that something so beautiful could come from a shell hidden on the bottom of the sea. Jesus called this most precious treasure the kingdom of heaven.

Early in my ministerial career, I was fascinated by the kingdom of heaven. For most of humanity, heaven is the place where God dwells, a home we hope to inhabit after death, but for Jesus it is much more.

One third of Jesus' ministry is about the kingdom. This is what got my attention. If heaven is God's dwelling place and where we go after we die, why is a third of Jesus' ministry dedicated to teaching us about the kingdom? Why is the kingdom the first thing He addressed when He began His service to humanity? There must be more to the kingdom than what religion teaches. It must be a great treasure for humanity, a pearl of great price, but are we willing to pay the price to have it?

The kingdom of heaven or the kingdom of God, as it is often called, is a forgotten kingdom reduced to a place where we go when we die, when, in fact, it is the pearl of great price. I saw this as a young minister and decided to explore all the parables (more than 30) and multiple statements that Jesus made about the kingdom heaven/kingdom of God to see if I could understand what it is. I concluded the kingdom of heaven is consciousness, specifically a consciousness of the First Light, an awareness of God.

Jesus' parables and statements help us understand the nature and value of a consciousness of truth. In the parables and statements, He reveals not only the nature of consciousness, but the inner journey of one who desires to experience the full value of the treasure.

The Field

The treasure is consciousness, and the field where it is "hidden" is our own being. Jesus revealed this "location" for the kingdom when He proclaimed that the kingdom is within us. Isn't it amazing that sometimes the greatest gifts are those so close to us that we cannot see them? We gaze afar when what we need is near. We climb mountains, descend into the depths of the sea and send probes into the vastness of space, when the greatest, most far-reaching discoveries await our inner journey.

Consider...to be, to live, is to be conscious, to know I am. All we know is known through our consciousness; all actions flow from our consciousness. Consciousness is the great treasure because it is the seed that contains all the possibilities; it is the womb that gives birth to all things, so let us explore the universe if we must, but now is the time to understand that the pearl of great price is consciousness, and there is *no where* we need to go, for the kingdom is *now here.*

Consciousness As A Seed

The first law of creation is "like begets like," and the first manifestation of this law is a seed. Seeds appear lifeless and without merit, but within their tiny confines is a vast potential. From a tiny mustard seed comes a plant that Jesus applauded and compared to faith. From an acorn rises a majestic oak and from a kernel of corn successive harvests can feed the world. From a microscopic sperm and egg is born a being able to experience the wonder of the First Light and Its creation, a being destined to let the light shine.

Consciousness, like a seed, bears fruit—some of it sweet and tender, some of it bitter and hard. Consciousness calls itself creator, maker and mother. Through the ages, it names itself writer, artist, musician, sculptor, baker, and builder.

Physicists who study the depths of the atom discovered that consciousness can bring what is possible into manifestation. Potential in the form of a wave "collapses" when perceived by consciousness and particles form. The writers of the Hindu ancient texts wrote of matter's dance stepping into form only to step back into formlessness. Our physicists confirm the Hindu wisdom, for throughout the cosmos particles and energy dance to the music of the spheres. A particle appears and then disappears only to appear again as if it cannot decide whether its destiny is to be a wave or a particle, to be a possibility or a reality.

Space is not empty, and one day we will unlock the potential that permeates this supposed void, but the lock will spin only when we realize the key is consciousness; only consciousness, only awareness, only knowing, only observation can collapse the wave and make what is possible live as a reality. Then unlimited energy and power will provide all we physically need, but this will occur only after we understand the nature of the First Light and our own being.

From Seed to Harvest

All that can be lives in us as our consciousness experiences desires and ponders possibilities. All that comes into being is the creation of consciousness and its desires, wonderings, ponderings, and curiosity. Consciousness is the great treasure because it is the seed that contains all possibilities; it is the womb that gives birth to all things.

In 2006 when I arrived in Fort Myers, Florida to serve the people of Unity of Fort Myers, I discovered a congregation yearning to grow and to build a new sanctuary. A seed had sprouted. The wave was collapsing.

It took years, but eventually what was held in mind and heart took shape and form. The first form was the vision of a group of people who asked what was needed to serve the people of the spiritual community. Next, an architect's rendering gave form to the vision of the space that was needed, and then blueprints were created to guide the builders.

In preparation for the new sanctuary, the congregation built a labyrinth defined by crushed shells and river rock. During a joyous ceremony, the people of the congregation took stones and wrote on the bottom of each rock words such as love, peace, God, joy, and phrases such as God is enough and have faith. These inscribed stones with the words facing down were placed on the ground forming the seven-circuit labyrinth. It bound the people to an ancient tradition, and day by day, the congregation walked the ancient circle in silence. Day by day, the words written on the bottom of the stones seeped into the earth, making holy ground where the new sanctuary would be built.

Then the day of the ground-breaking came. People gathered for song, celebration, and to declare a strange truth, "Nothing needs to happen," and from their willingness to let go, they created in their consciousness new possibilities of what could be. Doubt and concern fell away. There was peace. "Nothing needs to happen" created a peace that was the perfect companion for possibilities.

What was once an urge, a seed, became a consciousness that created a grand building where lives are transformed and consciousness grows. The walls, floor, and ceiling of the sanctuary set forth the presence of God in which the people continue to live, move, and have their being.

It is a beautiful story, a true story, of how consciousness is a seed-bearing fruit, a joyous, bountiful harvest, but not all seeds bring happiness and more possibilities. Some seeds of consciousness insure a harsh reality—pain and limitation.

As a minister I encountered people in varied states of consciousness. Their states of mind were seeds bearing fruit in their lives. Consider people who never admit a mistake, always blame others for their life conditions, and who think of themselves as victims.

This consciousness can cause grave problems—stagnation and arrested development, but new seeds can be planted. The beginning is a willingness to admit one's mistakes. At first, we may not be able to admit to ourselves or another the mistakes we have made, but willingness is a viable first step. It prepares the ground for new possibilities.

When we ponder our lives, admit our mistakes, and wonder about possibilities, our consciousness becomes a womb pregnant with possibilities that first take form as ideas. No one has ever seen an idea, but ideas are the foundation of all things. Then consciousness coalesces around the idea as a pearl forms around a grain of sand. In fact, one way the First Light makes Itself known in us is through ideas.

If you, dear friend, have a challenge in your life, do not look outside yourself for answers, look inside yourself and when you look, look for ideas. Ideas are the building blocks of consciousness and of creation. When cosmic consciousness becomes recognizable, it may first appear as an idea which like a seed must be watered and nurtured. Such is the way of creation.

Seeds As Possibilities

Seeds are mysterious. One Easter, Nancy and I were visiting one of our sons and his family. Ben and Leah wanted me to talk to Heidi, their daughter and our granddaughter, about Easter. She was quite young, so I did not want to confuse her by talking about Jesus, the cross and His passion and death and resurrection. That was for a later time. I chose to talk to her about Jesus' message to us about our potential.

I told her that Jesus could do incredible things. Not only did He bathe in water and drink water, He walked on water. Not only did He eat bread, but He made from a few loaves, bread for thousands of people who were hungry. He loved those who harmed Him. The most amazing thing I told her about Jesus was that He said we could do the things that He did and more. The most remarkable thing was that Jesus said we were like Him.

Next, I showed Heidi an apple and an apple seed, and I told her another surprising thing—that an apple was inside the seed. I grinned as she tried to press the apple into the seed, to no avail. I told her that we were like seeds and that within us was the possibility of doing great things. I told her that Jesus' message was that we could be like him. This was my first Jesus message to our granddaughter. It did not go well.

During a family FaceTime meeting, our granddaughter was talking to us and playing with her toys when she suddenly stopped and looked into the computer's camera and said, "Pop Pop, you were supposed to tell me about Jesus."

I replied, "I did tell you about Jesus. I told you that He said you could be just like him." Heidi wasn't buying it. Someone had told her about the cross, death, and resurrection. I am sure that in the years to come, we will talk about that Easter lesson and how an apple is in an apple seed. Needless to say, we have many interesting discussions in front of us.

Seeds are mysterious, and one of the great mysteries is how the seed of consciousness becomes our lives, how it manifests itself. This is our next area of exploration.

Law of Mind Action

All things begin as an idea. It is through ideas that consciousness expresses itself. An idea is like a plaything in the hand of a child. It is examined and explored. It is observed from every angle. It is tasted and touched, even smelled. It is shaken, and if a sound is heard it is shaken again and pressed to the child's ear. For adults, the examination of an idea is called thinking. Thoughts form around the idea; they are like the layers of nacre applied to a grain of sand by an oyster. An idea is a gathering place, a place that naturally attracts thoughts.

A great law is at work, the Law of Mind Action: *Thoughts held in mind produce after their kind.* This law simply states that when you think a thought, similar thoughts join in. If we continue to give them attention, if we hold them in mind, an attitude or belief forms. Beliefs are building blocks of consciousness, and consciousness is the formless out of which all is formed. Consciousness is the creator, the womb, but ideas, thoughts, attitudes, and beliefs are its raw material.

Beliefs are self-fulfilling prophecies. When we hold a certain belief, we find supporting evidence to reinforce the belief. If we think we are victims, we will find people willing to victimize us. If we believe we are failures, we will find a way to fail. If we are guilt-ridden, we will find a way to punish ourselves for our "sins."

Years ago, a woman counseled with me. She had been a nurse, but had not served in this way for many years; however, she loved nursing. Many years before, her actions had resulted in harm to a patient. Now she was feeling a desire to serve once more as a nurse. She was in school and doing well in her studies, but the closer she got to graduation, the more her past guilt asserted itself and plagued her.

She was so committed, knowledgeable, and competent that the only way she could fail was to skip the final exam. She came to see me the day she skipped the test. We talked about guilt and its associated belief in punishment. We had talked before about the past tragedy and the guilt she felt. Now it was time for her to break the pattern of punishment, pain, and self-inflicted limitation established by her consciousness of prolonged guilt.

With a focus on her heartfelt desire to serve again as a nurse, she called and asked the supervising nurse if she could take the exam at a later time. This was allowed, and I had the opportunity to be the guest speaker at her graduation.

All things do begin as an idea. Thoughts gather around an idea like the nacre that forms a pearl. Eventually, the thoughts harden into attitudes and beliefs that are added to our consciousness or awareness. Some of these "insights" are true, some are false, but whether they are true or false, they bear fruit. Every seed yields a harvest. Our consciousness becomes a life lived, our life.

More provisions for the journey….

1. Consciousness is the great treasure because it is the seed that contains all the possibilities; it is the womb that gives birth to all things.
2. Ideas are the building blocks of consciousness.
3. Thoughts held in mind produce after their kind; they form similar thoughts, related thoughts, that may evolve into attitudes and beliefs that shape our lives.

Come with me, the kingdom awaits. Not only is consciousness a treasure and a seed; it is an eye and a lamp.

CHAPTER EIGHT

The Eye and the Lamp

Gathering Light

When I was a young boy, I loved astronomy. I had a poster of the Solar System hanging over my bed. I knew the basic facts about each planet, what it was made of, how many astronomical units it was from the sun, its mass and how long it took to revolve on its axis and how many days it took to travel around the sun.

Many years later, Nancy and I built The High Meadow Observatory, a three-story structure housing a 14" telescope controlled by a computerized equatorial mount. I remember the day when a large crane arrived to lift and place the 10 foot rotating astronomical dome on top of the observatory. All the neighbors came to watch at our Sunrise Beach, Missouri home. I held my breath as many three-foot-long bolts secured the dome to the three-story wooden observatory.

With the completion of the observatory, it was time to calibrate the telescope and start collecting light. Since the time of Galileo, telescopes have gathered light. The light harvested by the telescope and magnified by its eyepiece entered the eyes and probing minds of cosmic seekers and changed the way we viewed our place in the universe. Our beliefs that the earth and humanity were the center of the universe were dashed by Galileo's observation of the moons of Jupiter, the moonlike phases of Venus, and Copernicus' book on the heliocentric solar system. Slowly our place in the universe was downgraded until today we inhabit a small planet in one of more than two trillion galaxies in the known universe.

Now not only do we gather light to observe the objects in our cosmic neighborhood, we study the light that is harvested from deep space. Light from a star, galaxy, or quasar can tell us about the movement of the heavenly body and the elements and compounds that constitute the object. One day, light from an exoplanet will tell us that the planet is suitable for human life and that we may have distant cousins who breathe air just as we do.

Little did I know as a child that my wondering about the night sky would become a yearning to gather the First Light, the light that came before the background cosmic microwave radiation found by radio astronomers Robert Wilson and Arno Penzias. Since the early years of my life, I have yearned to "see" the First Light and know the cosmic consciousness that gave birth to the universe. This light, this consciousness, is my quest, but it is only in recent years that I discovered the nature of my quest and my reason for being.

Consciousness As An Eye

We know consciousness is a treasure, and it is a seed that bears fruit, but it is also an eye, for it sees; like a telescope, it gathers light. Consciousness sees and knows the expanse of the universe from the microscopic and quantum domains to the seemingly limitless expansion of our cosmic home that is measured not by miles, but by using the speed of light as a measuring stick. Not only does the "eye" explore and see the physical universe; it explores ideas and their possibilities; it explores the formless out of which all is formed.

Consciousness explores itself. It gathers itself unto itself, and it does so in a unique way.

When consciousness gathers light, it observes. It does not judge, label or name. It simply sees. Consciousness aware of Itself declares, "I am that I am," and consciousness aware of what it sees says, "It is what it is." Later, through the five senses and the senses of the soul—wonder, curiosity, revelation, reflection, and thinking—what is observed and seen is known.

We are curious and full of wonder. We are children of the cosmos, eligible to enter the kingdom of God, but then we "grow up" and begin to name and label what we see. We no longer say, "It is what it is," instead we label it good or bad, and in doing so we arrest our ability to explore what is seen and to know its true nature. Rather than thoroughly explore what is observed, we study only one aspect of what is seen, or we explore only the outside of a thing rather than its interior. For instance, we think we are blood and body and fail to probe our psyche, thoughts, feelings, dreams, and visions. We think of one another as the words we speak and the things we do rather than our divine potential, a divine potential that only the First Light can reveal.

For instance, we say we have cancer when the fact is that the body contains cancer cells, but we are free of cancer and always shall be, for we are spiritual beings, expressions of the First Light, the light of the world.

Seeing Possibilities

The best teachers are those who look beyond a student's current status, behavior, and progress to what is possible. Once a teacher was given the IQ's of her students. It was an extraordinary class with great potential for advanced learning. One day, the principal spoke with the teacher about the class and how well the students were doing. The administrator informed the teacher that the class had far exceeded expectations, for the students had not done well in the past. The teacher told the principal that she was not surprised by their development because their IQ's were so high. The principal seemed puzzled. As the teacher and the principal continued to talk, they discovered that the teacher had been given not the student's intelligence quotients, but their locker numbers. However, the teacher's awareness of their "superior intelligence" called an unrealized potential into expression.

What I Have Seen

Consciousness is like an eye, for it observes; it has the capacity to see the surface of people and things and to judge by appearances, but consciousness can also be a probe that looks beyond the periphery to see capacity and potential.

This is the great joy of ministry; witnessing people living in limitation who lift their eyes from the ground and notice the mountains around them; witnessing people living in despair and anger, blaming others for their life condition and thinking of themselves as victims who begin to assume responsibility for their thoughts, attitudes, feelings, circumstances, and behavior. Over forty years of ministry, I saw this happen again and again. One person in particular comes to mind—Marilyn Webb.

When I met Marilyn, she was an unhappy-looking person who did not know the truth about herself. She was in a relationship that limited her life, but she possessed the qualities of the First Light. She was a seeker, a wonderer. She was a good person, intelligent, and when she heard the truth about her spiritual identity, she instinctively knew it was true. Her eye, her consciousness, opened to this new light; seeds were planted and a treasure was discovered. Now she is one of the most caring and positive people I know. In reminiscing about her transformation, I reminded her that she once looked forlorn, but now she was aglow with the beauty of the First

Light. We reminisce about the past and chuckle, and rejoice in what revelation can do. It is an honor to have been a part of her life and to know that she is one of the lights of the world.

One World, One Inhabitant

Consciousness is an eye that gathers light. It observes, but it is also like a glass through which we see, for we see the world, not as it is, but as we are. If the glass, the consciousness, is smudged or scratched, or if the eye is diseased, what we see and come to know are distorted. We fail to understand ourselves, others and our world. A vast vista is before us, but we look through a veil and see dimly and are often mystified by people who see a different world.

Police officers are aware of the varied ways eyewitnesses see the same event. We tend to think there is only one way to see an object, person or happening—our way—but this denies consciousness as an eye and as a glass through which we see. What we see and know reveals the state of our consciousness and the thoughts and attitudes that we hold in mind. Each of us lives in our own world, a world in which there is only one inhabitant.

2020 was an election year and like all election years, the revelation that consciousness is a glass was front and center. Members of opposing political parties seemed to live in different countries. 2020 was a year of "alternative facts," "fake news," and conspiracy theories. Consciousness as a window through which to see the world was on full display.

Consciousness Limited and Limitless

Each state of consciousness has its limits, a horizon that restricts its vision. When we stand in a valley, our sight is limited by the height of our eyes above the ground and the surrounding mountains and obstacles such as trees that obscure our line of sight. However, if we climb the surrounding summits, the horizon marches away from us and the extent of our vision expands. In the valley, we see only a few hundred feet in front of us while a view from a mountain top allows us to see for miles.

While attending West Jefferson High School in Harvey, Louisiana, I had a friend, Larry Sides, who was on the school's tennis team. He knew I had never played tennis, so, as a joke, he entered me in the school's tennis tournament. I decided to go along with the joke and play in the tournament. Remarkably, I won my first match. The second match I played a member of the tennis team and lost 8-3, but the coach, Doc Pete Riehl, watched the match and invited me to try out for the team.

By the next year, my senior year, I was the number one player on the team and had won a tourney, making me the best high-school tennis player on the west bank of the New Orleans metropolitan area.

During my senior year, the team traveled to Baton Rouge, Louisiana for an away match. I played against a boy who was ranked seventh in the south. As the match began, I thought there was no way I could beat such a player. As a matter of fact, I had seen him play doubles at the state championship a year earlier when I was a junior in high school. Remembering his play that day did not bolster my confidence for the match in Baton Rouge. However, the first set of the match was close. Eventually, my horizon expanded from losing to winning, and I won the match in three sets. Later in the year, he and his team came to New Orleans for a return match, and I won again.

While attending high school, I knew nothing of consciousness, but looking back I see how consciousness is not only a seed that bears fruit, but a glass through which we see ourselves and our capabilities, and it is evident that consciousness can change in the course of a few minutes.

Doc Riehl became an important influence on my life. He was not a member of the faculty of West Jefferson High School. He was a practicing physician who loved tennis and who loved helping boys discover themselves through this life-long sport. As my junior year of high school and my first season of tennis drew to a close, Doc talked to me and my parents about a summer job working as a tennis counselor at Camp Menatoma near Augusta, Maine. I would be gone for most of the summer, and I would gain experience teaching other young boys how to play tennis.

In my years at Camp Menatoma, not only did I teach tennis, I led mountain trips to Mount Katadhin, the northern terminus of the Appalachian Trail, Mt. Washington in the Presidential mountain range in New Hampshire as well as other mountains in Maine. I spent five summers in Maine at the camp and came to love Maine… in the summer. I even won the Central Maine State Championship one year. One of the matches was particularly interesting. It was another example of a shift in consciousness.

I was playing against the number one seed, the person expected to win the tournament. I was unseeded because no one knew who I was or my past record in tennis. The tournament officials were unaware that I attended Old Dominion College on a tennis scholarship and played number one for the team. The first set went quickly because I lost it, 6 games to love. In other words, zero games for me, six for him. And then something happened. A shift occurred in consciousness. I entered the zone. The ball slowed down, I was hitting miraculous shots, and I won the second set 6 games to love and the third set as well. All athletes strive for the zone, a consciousness that bears fruit as superior performance. The next day, I won the championship match in straight sets.

Doc taught me tennis. He helped me with my strokes, took me to a Czechoslovakian Davis Cup player to look at my game, but it was Doc's countenance that was most instructive. He was calm and peaceful. I never saw him rattled. He never raised his voice. I think I often modeled his consciousness when I played. It was an invitation to be in the moment, but not all moments are the zone.

Many years after high school and college, Nancy and I lived in Albany, Georgia. I was in the Navy, flying in RA5C reconnaissance jets. I still loved tennis and thrived on the competition. Each year I played in the city championships. One year, my doubles partner and I won the city doubles championship, and immediately following the doubles match, I played in the singles championship. It was a close match. During the third and final set, my legs cramped, and I fell to the ground in agony. I was dehydrated from two back-to-back matches in the hot, humid Georgia summer.

People rushed on the court to help me. Eventually, the pain subsided and I was able to stand, but I was hobbled and found that whenever I pushed off the ground with my legs while serving, the cramps and crippling pain returned. My only way to compete was to serve underhand.

I knew I could not continue to play much longer, so I started going for winners at every opportunity. It was consciousness at work again. Through the veil, I saw a path to victory, and I walked—actually I hobbled—toward it, and it worked. I won.

Consciousness is like a seed, and we determine what kind of seed is planted and therefore the harvest that is to come. Consciousness is like a glass through which we see, and we can rise up and see vast possibilities that others may not be able to see. We gather light and if we do so without judgment, our ability to live in the moment allows the First Light to shine with its possibilities.

Consciousness As A Lamp

Consciousness is like an eye, enabling us to see. The eye can gather the light of truth or the darkness of error. Likewise, consciousness is like a glass, window or a veil through which we see. The glass can be clear and our vision true, it can be cloudy or blurry because the window through which we view ourselves, others and the world is tainted, or consciousness can be like a lamp radiating light or darkness. Jesus knew that consciousness could expand our vision or obscure it. It could be a light to the world or cast long, dark shadows.

> *"The lamp of the body is the eye. If therefore your eye is good your whole body will be full of light, but if your eye is bad, your whole body will be full of darkness. If therefore the light that is in you is darkness, how great is that darkness."*
>
> Matthew 6:22-23

Jesus had a unique view of the eye. Not only does the eye gather light, it shines light like a lamp, and amazingly the "light" can actually be darkness. In other words, our consciousness radiates; it expresses itself. We are called to be the light of the world, but we are capable of radiating darkness, negativity and error. Here is the truth—what is within us, we radiate into the world. What we see and come to believe does not remain in us; it is like a lamp that illumines our world and determines what we see. What is seen in the world is actually a part of us.

We may think what we see is outside of us, but it is not true. What we see is gathered light radiating from within us. Remember the rock on the path? We may see it and step over it or trip over it, but in either circumstance, it is a part of our consciousness and therefore a part of us. We think the stone is on the path, but it is closer than we think, for whatever we see or know is a part of our consciousness. The more aware we are, the more we see and the more we know. The higher we stand, the clearer our vision and the more radiant the light we shine.

> *"You are the light of the world. A city that is set on a hill cannot be hidden. Nor do they light a lamp and put it under a basket, but on a lampstand, and it gives light to all who are in the house. Let your light so shine before men, that they may see your good works, and glorify your Father in heaven."*
>
> Matthew 5:14-16

Each of us is a beacon radiating our consciousness—thoughts, feelings, attitudes and beliefs—as either light or darkness. Jesus called us to be lights of the world, not darkness. The light that shines or the consciousness that radiates and manifests itself is to be such that people know it is not personal consciousness at work. The life we live is to be a life that is an expression of the First Light, a manifestation of God. We become transparent, invisible men, women, and children, for what stands on the hill or the lampstand is the light God is.

Its Mantra

Consciousness, like a seed, grows and bears fruit. Like begets like is its mantra. The consciousness like an eye gathers light and sees. What we see is within us is its mantra. Consciousness like a window is the veil through which we perceive and understand. We see through the veil dimly, is its mantra. Consciousness like a lamp illumines the world. We are the light of the world is its mantra.

The seed, the eye, and the lamp are paired with the eating of the fruit of the Tree of the Knowledge of Good and Evil. This is evident, for the world we often see is a world of conflict and war. Battlefields abound: Theopolis, Waterloo, Yorktown, Gettysburg, Bastogne, Normandy. Other fields of conflict are the United States Congress, Great Britain's Parliament and Wall Street. Light and darkness are glorified in the books we read and the movies we watch. Time and time again, people and ideologies are pitted against one another. We eat of the Tree of Knowledge of Good and Evil, we name people foes and demons, and the seeds of conflict sprout and grow. The eye sees what is within it, and when it looks upon the world, it sees a projection of itself. Like a lamp, it radiates whatever "light" burns within us.

It is strange that from the seed, the eye, and the lamp can come both war and peace. However, when we enter the consciousness of the First Light, there is no conflict, no fear, and no separation. All are united and have their place.

H. Emilie Cady, who wrote Unity's first book, *Lessons In Truth*, once gathered light that formed these words in her mind: "There is no evil." This does not mean there was no Holocaust. It means there is a state of consciousness where there is no evil. In fact, there is no good either, but there are possibilities.

Consciousness is a hand that sows seeds, an eye that gathers light and observes, and a lamp shining high on a hill. Like the intersection of crossroads, the hand, the eye, and the lamp are one and are called by the same name—consciousness. The seeds sown can feed the world or cause famine; the eye can gather truth or error and the lamp can be a beacon of the First Light or the darkest of nights.

More provisions for the journey…

1. Consciousness is an eye that sees best when it gathers light without judgment or condemnation.
2. Each of us lives in our own world, a world in which there is only one inhabitant.
3. Consciousness is a glass, a veil, through which we see dimly.
4. Consciousness is a lamp that illumines our life and our world.

The facets of the jewel that is consciousness glisten. They are treasure and seed, eye and lamp, but there is more. Come with me, for there is a pond into which we must drop a pebble.

CHAPTER NINE

Pebble In The Pond

Child's Play

I am sitting beside a pond. The water is still, reflecting the sky and surroundings. I skip flat stones across the surface and count the number of times each stone touches the water. I try to increase the touches by lowering the trajectory of the stone and by throwing it faster. It is child's play filled with fun and anticipation, but then I do a new thing, something more contemplative, with only the pull of gravity at work. I drop a pebble in the pond. Ripples emanate from the point where the pebble enters the water. Circular waves surround the point of entry and travel to the shore. Consciousness is like a pebble perpetually dropped into a pond, causing ripples in space-time, ripples called life.

Metaphysicians tend to think consciousness causes events and circumstances, but long before something happens in the world, long before the ripples reach the shore, the creative mark of consciousness is evident for those with eyes to see, with ears to hear and with the sensitivity to know what moves within them. In the beginning, ripples are on the surface of the pond, but there are no events or circumstances. What is happening is not happening in the world; it is happening in us.

It is true that consciousness contributes to circumstances, but the events of our lives are made possible by the intersection of ripples caused by multiple pebbles entering the water. In truth, the collective consciousness, or the consciousness of the human race, is perpetually creating global events. In addition, there is the melding of the collective consciousness of families, businesses, and even the intersection of ripples on a pond caused by two friends who talk into the night about the meaning of life and their dreams for the future. Ripples abound, ensuring there is no still water on the global pond. I concede that consciousness contributes to events globally, nationally, locally, and personally; however, this is far from the whole truth.

Long before there is an event in the world, ripples traverse our being, for the first creation of personal consciousness is thought, and when a thought is held in mind, it attracts similar thoughts that join to become attitudes and beliefs. More ripples emerge from the point of entry of the pebble, and feelings are felt. A life is made manifest. Usually, the consciousness and its manifestation are far from pure, but the principle is the same—pebble in the pond, consciousness creating ripples that first occupy our minds and then the world. The question is, who drops the pebble and what is the nature of the stone.

A Pebble of Light

Usually, we bend down and pick up a pebble from the shore, and then we toss it in the pond, but perhaps it is possible for the pebble to come from a more distant shore, a different source. Perhaps the pebble is not made of common thoughts, attitudes, and beliefs, but is a revelation, a pebble of light, an emanation of the First Light. Such ripples create a new life, a life never lived before.

My new life began when I was in high school. My family lived in Gretna, Louisiana on the west bank of the Mississippi River across from New Orleans. Often when we went to the Big Easy, we drove down St. Charles Street with its mansions and an oddly shaped building called Unity Temple. This structure of interlocking circles captured our attention. It was the topic of many family conversations.

One day when I returned home on a semester break from college, my parents informed me that the oddly shaped building was a church and that I should attend with them next Sunday. I agreed and two things struck me. First, the minister was a woman, Rev. Ruth Murphy. I had never seen a female minister before. Second, that Sunday nearly the whole service was a Lord's Supper or spiritual communion, but there were no elements of bread or wine. The service was a meditative experience, and it moved me. After the service, I bought my first Unity book, *Lessons In Truth*, by H. Emily Cady. The ideas were new to me, but I was fascinated by them.

After graduation from Old Dominion College with a degree in Chemistry, I joined the aviation branch of the Navy. On Valentine's Day, 1970, while still an aviation officer candidate, I asked Nancy to marry me. She kept me in suspense when she answered, "Let me think about it." A moment later she said yes. What a great day. I remember the two of us crammed in a phone booth calling my parents to tell them the news. On June 20, 1970, we were married in Nancy's home church. I took my bride with me to Pensacola where I completed my basic aviation training. Next, I attended an intense flight program in Brunswick, Georgia where I received my Naval Flight Officer wings. Now it was time to really fly; it was time to join the fleet.

My orders sent me to the Ready Air Group (RAG), RVAH-3, in Albany, Georgia where I received specialized training in operating the reconnaissance systems in the back cockpit of the fleet aircraft. I would fly more than 100 combat missions over North Vietnam. The RA5C was a supersonic reconnaissance jet that gathered intelligence through film, infrared, passive electronic measures as well as side-looking-radar. Initially, this aircraft was designated A3J, and it was designed as a carrier-based nuclear bomber. Research from the X-15 went into the turning surfaces and computers of this supersonic aircraft. The nuclear weapon was carried inside the aircraft behind fuel tanks. To launch the weapon, the pilot executed a maneuver allowing the spent fuel tanks to be ejected followed by the deployment of the bomb. There was only one problem…sometimes the fuel tanks got hung up and were not ejected. Not good. The pilot and attack officer were then riding an armed nuclear weapon they could not deploy.

The Navy had a supersonic carrier-based aircraft without a mission. Eventually, it became a reconnaissance platform that performed thousands of highly productive missions, many of them over Vietnam, others monitoring Soviet forces in Cuba.

On one of the training missions at RVAH-3, Commander Ron Polfer and I flew to Richards-Gebaur Air Force near Independence, Missiouri where his parents lived. We visited them and stayed overnight at their home. In the morning as Commander Polfer's parents prepared to take us to our plane for our return flight to Albany, Georgia, I asked if Unity Village was nearby. (Unity Village is the world headquarters of the Unity Movement.) To my surprise, they informed me it was on the way to Richards-Gebaur Air Force Base. I remember seeing the famous Unity Tower for the first time as we approached the campus that would become my spiritual home.

I made two other trips to Unity Village while I was in the Navy. The second trip, Ken Storms and I were on our way to display a RA5C at an airshow in Yuma, Arizona and stopped overnight at Richard-Gebaur Airforce Base. I had a meeting the next day at the Village to talk with Rev. Phil White about becoming a Unity Minister. Ken and I ate supper at the Officer's Club, had a bottle of wine and went to a bar in the club where we proceeded to take on the Air Force officers in a friendly game of shuffle bowling. The winners got free drinks. We won most of the games, and late in the evening, I was Navy drunk, if you know what I mean. Somehow it dawned on me that I had an interview the next day to talk about becoming a minister. I went to my room and passed out. I woke up in bad shape. I remember standing in the shower with the water pounding on my face thinking, "what have I done?"

Richard and Marilyn Rieger, both ministerial students at Unity School of Religious Studies, picked me up to take me to my interview. I was excited to talk to them, but I tried not to breathe on them, for obvious reasons. Rev. Phil White and I met. Since I had little Unity experience, he recommended that I get a dozen Unity books and read them. After our meeting, I went to the bookstore on campus and purchased the books. I took them with me on a ten-month combat cruise to Vietnam. It was interesting reading spiritual books while being in combat nearly every day.

When I returned home from Vietnam and took a well-earned vacation, Nancy and I attended a Rose Festival Retreat at Unity Village. One of the days, Nancy attended the retreat activities, and I interviewed with the hope of being admitted into ministerial school. There was no Unity church in Albany, Georgia where the Navy reconnaissance air wing was stationed, so when I went for my Unity interviews, I had only attended half a dozen Sunday services and no classes necessary for admittance into the ministerial program.

One of my interviews was with Rev. Ed Rabel, a master Bible metaphysician who became my faculty advisor when I was in school. I saw my application on his desk. It was covered with red ink. He began, "You don't know much about Unity, do you?"

I answered, "No, sir, I don't."

He retorted, "Good; too many people come here thinking that they know everything."

I said, "That won't be me."

I interviewed throughout the day meeting faculty members and other giants within the Unity Movement. I was excited. Nancy was not.

Long before attending the Rose Festival Retreat at Unity Village, I remember sitting in bed with Nancy reading *Lessons In Truth*. I looked at her and said, "I think I am going to become a Unity minister."

She looked at me as only Nancy can look at me and replied, "You're crazy." Obviously, Nancy was not keen on me leaving the Navy and becoming a minister.

I said, "Why don't you read *Lessons In Truth*, and we can talk about it." Nancy read the book and couldn't find a thing to disagree with, and this troubled her even more.

When we arrived at Unity Village for the Rose Festival Retreat, Nancy expected to be transformed as we entered the gates. It did not happen. She thought everyone at the Village was ancient. (We were both in our mid-twenties.) She was disturbed and more convinced than ever that this was a bad idea.

One afternoon, during "Me" time, time when there was no retreat program, Nancy and I played tennis. She was thinking, *God if you want us to do this, you have got to give me a sign because I am not on board with what is happening.* Nancy missed a shot and the ball rolled off the court. She went to get it. The ball was on a patch of bare ground. Right next to it was a four-leaf clover. Nancy took this as her sign, and from that moment on the people at the Village started looking younger. We still have that four-leaf clover. It is in a framed copy of James Dillet Freeman's poem, *I Am There*, a copy of which is on the moon.

After returning home, I received more questions from the ministerial school. I quickly answered them and returned them to the Unity School of Religious Studies. While my answers were in transit, I received a letter from the School. I remember Nancy calling me at work telling me that an official-looking letter had arrived from Unity. I asked her to open it. She was reluctant to open it and read it over the phone because she knew it was about my admittance into the program. She opened it and read it to me. I was in.

This is the mystery of consciousness, of pebbles dropping into the pond. I dropped some of the pebbles, but life is not that simple. Life is an intersection of lives and an overlapping of ripples on the pond. Always, there is mystery.

This is our potential. Consciousness develops, but much of it is unknown to us. A potential is created, actually a destiny comes into being, but there is a problem. We judge by appearances. In the case of my entry into ministry, I was too naïve to be deterred by appearances or my lack of experience in Unity. I forged ahead with no regard to appearances. I was fortunate to be admitted to Unity School of Religious Studies.

During my second deployment prior to entering ministerial school, I testified before a congressional committee aboard ship about why I was leaving the Navy. I was a distinguished naval graduate from Aviation Officer School, and therefore my naval officer commission was designated regular instead of reservist. This enabled me to resign my commission before the completion date on my contract with the government and to enter the ministerial class of 1976.

Judge Not By Appearances

It is important to know ourselves. There is a divinity about us. The vibration of creation clings to us—*I am that I am.* This is pure consciousness. We are the first creation of this Consciousness; we are individualized expressions of the awakened universe. The Creator gathered light, consciousness, and gave us our first words to speak, *"I am."* We are made, but we are also makers.

We stand on the shore and gather pebbles that make us creatures of the earth, human beings, and in doing so we forget we are *lights of the world.* Instead, we believe we are clods of dirt. We judge by appearances. We focus on events, happenings, and circumstances and think they are the building blocks of our lives. They are not.

Jesus cautioned us, "Do not judge according to appearances…" (John 7:24). We are not to make decisions and draw conclusions based solely on what appears, for we can be deceived. We live in a magical place where things appear and disappear and fail to realize that a magical world is a world of illusion.

Hopefully, events are not the source of our knowledge and understanding, but they can be. Experience is a hard teacher. Ideally, our classroom is still water, and our teacher is a pebble from a distant shore, but when we are unaware of what moves in us, there is no stillness. The pebble may enter the water again and again, but we give little credence to the thoughts and feelings that rush to the shore. Thoughts are simply thoughts, and feelings are either something to enjoy, shed, or to suppress. We do not understand that thoughts and feelings are the first creation of our consciousness. They are the first ripples on the pond. We are unaware. We have consciousness, but we are not conscious.

By Their Fruits

We breathe and our skin is warm, but we are not alive. We exist without awareness; however, there is a way to know the depth of our being and a way to become acquainted with the ripples that are reflected time and time again within us. "You will know them by their fruits" (Matthew 7:16).

We know people and their character by what they do. Their actions are their fruits. For instance, lying is a fruit, as is cheating. Caring for those in need is a fruit. Some fruits cast seeds that are a blight on the land, and other fruits cast seeds that yield an abundant harvest that feeds the best parts of us and encourages others. However, knowing ourselves requires a more detailed discovery of the first ripples that enter the pond. We see the obvious, the things we do and other people do, but there is a secret part of us—thoughts, attitudes, beliefs, intentions, images, dreams, and feelings. Our consciousness must not be an unexplored land, for when we do not know ourselves, we do not know what we do. It is as Jesus said as He hung on the cross, "...they do not know what they do" (Luke 23:34).

Not knowing the ramifications of our actions and consistent behavior is a central problem for humanity, but the greater problem is that we do not know what causes what we do. These first ripples on the pond or expressions of consciousness bear fruit, and it is these fruits that we must come to know—thoughts, attitudes, beliefs, intentions, perceptions, and feelings. Often the knowing is painful, for these beliefs about ourselves, others and the world formed during times of trauma and pain.

Know Thyself

The journey beyond the god of dogma requires that we know our secret self. We usually proceed in two ways. First, we wait until the ripples of our consciousness strike the shore and show up as events, happenings, or situations. These circumstances often reveal secret, unknown parts of us that are at work in our lives. This is the age-old method of trial-and-error, and it is filled with pain. The happenings point us within, but we may not venture into this cave because of pain and irresponsibility. The result is that the circumstance repeats itself. A pattern forms in the world because of the consistency of our consciousness and its thoughts, perceptions, attitudes, beliefs, and intentions. And most painful of all—the feelings repeat themselves, and we are afraid of them; we are afraid of ourselves.

Another relationship ends. We are betrayed, and the betrayal reinforces our belief that we are victims. We fear our feelings and may eventually fear relationships. What is worse, loneliness, or the pain of a failed relationship? Another job is lost. It begins with promise, but it ends like all the other jobs we have lost, with confusion, anger, and blame. We begin to doubt our abilities and our secret thought is there is something wrong with us. There is darkness about us, and we want nothing to do with it, but ignoring the secret self is to betray our humanity and to never discover its role in our journey beyond god.

The Cave

We stand at the entrance to our secret selves. The opening of the cave is dark. We turn away, filled with anger, resentment, and blame. We pace back and forth in front of the blackness. We step toward the entrance of the cave, but we cannot bring ourselves to step inside. It is as if the entrance is guarded by some unknown presence.

It is true; the cave is guarded. There are sentries unknown to us—guilt, regret, and the devil. This devil is not an entity opposing God. It is the personification of our irresponsibility. We are unwilling to consider our role in our failed relationships or sputtering career. We are familiar with blame, but unaware of our irresponsibility, guilt, and regret, and therefore we cannot enter the cave, the seeming darkness of our being.

A pebble from a distant shore, a revelation, is dropped into our pond. It is the realization that it is our pond, our consciousness, and that we are responsible for our thoughts, feelings, and actions. As soon as this pebble enters the pond, ripples of guilt and regret course through us. The healing is beginning. These feelings are the beginning of the self-aware person, but there is danger.

Regret when suppressed can becomes depression. Guilt without forgiveness can cause us to punish ourselves with more failure, but regret and guilt combined with acceptance can heal us. But notice what enables us to enter into our own being, to become acquainted with our secret self—responsibility.

A responsible person takes the hands of guilt and regret and steps into the darkness of the cave and finds there is light. We see dimly, but we see. On the floor of the cave are dark stones.

Dark Stones

Not everything that is precious glitters. Most of us could not recognize a diamond in the rough. Some of the most valuable substances first appear as ore that must be refined. We pick up a dark stone, perhaps a memory of a traumatic event, abuse, rape, hurtful actions on our part, etc. We see in the stone the memory of what happened or what we did, what we said or what was said to us, and then we remember that this time was when our self-demeaning thoughts and beliefs came into being. Strong feelings came alive that paralyzed us. This was when it began.

This knowing ignites a fire that refines the ore that reveals its precious parts. Valuable insights and realizations emerge. The stone becomes molten. We think it is too hot or painful to hold, but in this plasma state, it can be reshaped. New beliefs can form. We can accept what happened, what we did, and what we chose to believe about ourselves. The healing is under way.

Forgiveness

Responsibility, regret, and guilt are prerequisites for one of the greatest leaps in spiritual awareness—forgiveness. Forgiveness may appear to be about the person who has wronged us, but this is not true. When asked how many times we should forgive, Jesus answered, "I do not say to you, up to seven times, but up to seventy times seven" (Matthew 18:22). Obviously, if we have to forgive someone 490 times, the forgiveness is not affecting the other person. Does this mean we have to keep forgiving until the other person "gets it?" No, we forgive until *we* get it.

The hidden truth about forgiveness is this: all forgiveness is self-forgiveness. A woman may ask, "Why should I forgive myself when I was brutally raped? Do I need to forgive myself when a white supremacist murdered my son?"

My grievances have not been as acute as rape and murder, but I have struggled with this same question. Why must I forgive myself when I was the person wronged? Imagine resting in prayer and meditation feeling hurt and betrayed and this pebble is dropped into your pond: *forgive yourself.* For what? The answer comes, and my humanity is less rigid, more malleable, better able to be molded and sculpted by an emerging consciousness. *You must forgive yourself for the thoughts of anger, rage, hatred, or revenge that fill your consciousness. The pain of the event has passed, but the pain of your resentment remains, and if it continues it will taint if not solidify your consciousness. It will become rigid and the purpose for being, to become increasingly aware, will be forgotten.*

These are hard words, but they are true. Truth ignites a fire that purifies, but the flames can hurt. Oh, how I have wanted people to pay a karmic debt for their actions, but with the installment of each payment, I was less.

So, I asked, "How do I forgive myself?" Here is what I learned.

First, forgiveness is a return to love. When we are resentful, filled with hate and thoughts of revenge, our hearts are closed. We cannot express our true nature, which is love. The other person may have spoken and acted with malice, but our thoughts, feelings, and beliefs foul our nest. Our indignation may be justified, but our feelings, thoughts, and beliefs are affecting our interior life, usually people around us and our life experience.

It is time to take the next step. We must become someone we have never been before, someone who was never harmed, someone who was never raped and whose son did not die at the hand of another. This was Jesus' teaching. Let me explain. Stay with me now….

As a minister I have married many couples. Many of the individuals were divorced. Jesus said that a divorced person cannot remarry without committing adultery. "Whoever divorces his wife and marries another commits adultery against her. And if a woman divorces her husband and marries another, she commits adultery" (Mark 10:11-12). How can this be? What did He mean?

Here is what I have shared in counseling prior to the marriage ceremony. I tell the couple about Jesus' statement and that it is relevant to them. Often when a person is divorced, there is much anger and resentment. These thoughts, feelings and negative beliefs about their spouse linger and continue to connect the divorced person to their divorced spouse.

There may be a court document that says they are no longer married, but a connection remains. They are not free. They are bound to their past spouse by their anger and resentment and the thoughts they hold in mind. **In fact**, they are divorced. **In truth**, they are still bound to one another, still married.

This is why Jesus said a divorced person cannot remarry. Only a new person, one that has grown in consciousness, can remarry. The court documents may say the person is divorced, but this is not true. By releasing anger and resentment, a new person is born who has never been married.

This is the key to forgiveness. We must become a person who was not harmed, not raped, nor betrayed. This new person has an open heart and can express the love that is the truth of being. The individual has the same name, but is new. Only self-forgiveness can grant us this gift. The heart opens, and we are born anew.

And what of the other person? He has before him the same path we must walk—self-forgiveness. It is the only way out of the darkness.

More provisions for the journey….

1. Consciousness is like a pebble dropped into a pond.
2. The ripples on the pond become the events and circumstances of our lives, but the first ripples are thoughts and feelings.
3. One of our problems is that we judge by appearances.
4. The things that happen in our lives can help us know what is happening in us. "By their fruits you shall know them."

5. The beginning of self-realization, another form of awareness, is responsibility. We must discover that we are the maker of our thoughts, feelings and actions. No more blame.
6. We must venture into the darkness of our being. The entrance to this cave is guarded by the devil (irresponsibility), regret, and guilt.
7. The beginnings of healing are responsibility and the courage to take the hands of guilt and regret and enter the cave. In the depth of our being we find dark stones, precious ore needing to be refined.
8. All forgiveness is self-forgiveness.

Come with me and let us become wicks in God's candle.

CHAPTER TEN

The Wick

Where Are We?

My journey beyond the god of religion made me a shepherd and took me to the slopes of Mount Horeb where I encountered the burning bush and God whose name is *I am that I am*. I discovered that God is consciousness. This is the image and likeness in which we are made. We are conscious beings. We are aware, and if we want to know the nature of our Creator, the nature of consciousness, then the place to begin our exploration is our own consciousness.

The expedition is under way. We know that consciousness is the pearl of great price; it is the greatest treasure, for to be aware is to be alive and to be alive is to become increasingly aware. This gives us purpose.

Gripping the treasure in our hands and pressing it to our hearts, we discovered another reason consciousness is precious; it is like a seed, for it produces after its kind. The first seeds were planted not in the earth, but in the fields of our minds. A thought held in mind produced similar thoughts that gathered and circled one another to become attitudes and beliefs.

Consciousness then formed an eye through which it saw the cosmos and our lives, but its sight was limited by attitudes and beliefs. These parts of ourselves limited our horizon; however, as our attitudes and beliefs changed, the world seemed to change, but did it? What is the source of our sight? Is it what is seen, the eye that sees, or the light it sees by? We are still trying to answer these questions.

One discovery was that consciousness not only sees; it shines. It is not only an eye; it is a lamp. It not only gathers light like a telescope, it emits light like a sun. Consciousness radiates, it casts its "light" so the eye can see. Consciousness either shrouds others in darkness or it shows the way.

As we become more aware, we become more sensitive to the light (consciousness) that others radiate. We can see the darkness behind a false smile. We can detect the insincerity of compliments. We can see the twinkle in the eye of someone who is also a shepherd and who has seen the burning bush we have seen.

Consciousness is a treasure; it is a seed producing after its kind; it sees, it radiates and it is a pebble dropped in a pond causing concentric circles that intersect with other ripples and become our lives.

This is where we are, but how did we get here? What impulses led humanity to discover that God is consciousness and that consciousness is a treasure, a seed, an eye, a veil, a lamp, and a pebble in a pond? Awe, wonder, and curiosity led the way.

"Look At That! What About That?"

We found the first evidence of life in fossils embedded in ancient rock, but we yearn to look farther back in time to find proof of a divine design, the first evidence of a Creator. But perhaps we should look at a more recent time to find evidence of the God we seek.

Awe, wonder, and curiosity are signs of a divine design and a Creator at work in us. We first became acquainted with awe, wonder, and curiosity when we were young. Sunsets and sunrises caused us to stop and stare, and tiny lights in the night invited us to lie on our backs and ponder. Clouds took shape and appeared as animals and forms in the sky. Bugs and butterflies were mysteries to us, and mountains called for us to climb them because they were there. We were more conscious, and the teachers that brought to our attention these marvels were awe, wonder, and curiosity. These teachers do not inform us, they simply said, "Look at that! What about that?"

As a child, awe and wonder were my friends. The words "Look at that! What about that" snapped my head and my mind from one thing to another. Curiosity took me to strange places and got me into trouble. It started with gunpowder.

When I was thirteen, I knew the three substances that constituted the explosive: charcoal, sulfur, and salt peter or potassium nitrate, but I didn't know the correct proportion of the ingredients causing the materials to burn with explosive power. I decided to conduct my own experiments to "invent" gunpowder. I combined the three substances in different proportions until I found a particularly explosive mixture. I tested it by placing a small amount of my concoction in a small glass bottle with a screw on cap. I drilled a hole in the cap and inserted a fuse. I placed the bottle at the top of the outdoor steps leading to my basement where I had my chemistry lab. (For the test of my gunpowder, the basement became a bunker.) I lit the fuse and dashed down the steps to the bunker and peered out the window of the basement door. The concoction ignited and to my dismay the bottle took off and headed toward our neighbor's yard where his dog rested peacefully. The bottle exploded, and the dog did not leave its doghouse for the rest of the day.

I had invented gunpowder. I wasn't the first, but as with the original inventor, awe, wonder, and curiosity led the way.

Next, I turned my attention to bugs. This is where young boys become cruel. I remember putting a bug in water and placing the insect and container in the freezer and leaving it overnight. The next day I thawed the ice, and the bug lived. I am glad that my cryogenic experiments ended, as I released the creature to tell his friends about the mystery of suspended animation.

Trouble became my middle name when I invented a way to kill insects with smoke. The device consisted of two metal coffee cans one above the other connected by a thin tube through which smoke traveled from the bottom tin where fire burned to the upper tin where the bug lay.

I started the fire in the basement and some of the smoke moved from the bottom tin to the top tin where the insect was placed, but most of the smoke filled the basement. The blower on the HVAC system came on and pulled the smoke into the rest of the house. My mother and father were preparing to go to church where my Dad was a part-time lay preacher, but the house appeared to be on fire. It was not, but my father, who had a fiery temper, was justifiably incensed. It was some time before I was allowed into my basement laboratory again, so I turned my attention to electronics.

Did you know you can make a radio with copper wire, the lead from a pencil and a razor blade? Soldiers in World War II built GI radios to listen to local radio stations. They really work. I made mine and decided to expand its reception by stretching an antenna wire from my upstairs bedroom window to the window of my friend who lived across the street. Everything was fine until a kid rode down the street on his bike flying a kite. The kite string struck my antenna and ripped my GI radio off my desk and out of my second story window. More trouble for me, but the power of awe, wonder, and curiosity was permanently etched in my soul, and, in fact, is driving me to write this book.

I graduated from Old Dominion College with a degree in Chemistry; however, my destiny was not to become a chemist but an explorer of the kingdom of heaven, something more elusive and mysterious than insects, cryo-engineering, explosives, and electronics.

Can you see the path we walk? Awe, wonder and curiosity witness our birth and are evidence of the presence of the Creator. These three companions stand beside our cribs and wait for the opportunity to say, "Look at that! What about that?" At first, we explore our surroundings. Everything goes in our mouths, but soon our other senses are engaged. Our consciousness expands and a few of us turn within to a kingdom more vast than the cosmos. A few of us discover that the God of the mountain is the God of the burning bush, the God that is consciousness, the One that calls Itself, *I am that I am.*

We may explore our surroundings and contribute to a growing awareness of the universe, but the kingdom of consciousness is the ultimate discovery. Its siren call is awe and wonder. All children hear this call, and they heed the sweet voice of curiosity, "Look at that! What is that?" But, often, as adults we no longer incline our ear to these simple words. We become jaded, and no longer see shapes in clouds or pause to allow an insect its rite of passage. Sunrise and sunset are ignored, and seldom do we see the twinkle of stars in the night sky.

Perhaps this is why Jesus said, "Let the children come to Me, and do not forbid them, for such is the kingdom of heaven" (Matthew 19:14). Who are the children? Is their main characteristic the few years they have circled the sun, or is it their inclination to hear the voice of awe and wonder, "Look at that! What is that?" The young may crawl because they have not yet learned to walk, or they have circled the sun many times and now walk with a cane. The young give no credence to age; they pledge allegiance to the need to become increasingly aware. This is the driving force of the God that is consciousness.

I am blessed, for I still hear the voice of awe and wonder and feel the pull of curiosity. They are the sweetest of sounds and the most endearing signs that there is a Creator, and the Creator is consciousness.

The Wick

It is Sunday morning, and I stand before those I serve. I am in the midst of my talk. I ask for two volunteers to come forward. Two women stand before me. They introduce themselves to the congregation. I give one person a small, unlit votive candle, and I give the other person a box of matches. I ask the person with the matches to light the candle. The match is struck, a flame burns, and the volunteer's candle is lit. Then I ask the person with the match to light a votive candle I hold in my hand. It does not light. The person tries again, but to no avail.

I ask, "What's wrong?" (I suggest to the person with the match that she blow out the flame, so as not to burn herself.)

She answers, "There is no wick in the candle."

"Is that a problem?" I ask. The volunteer's nod says yes.

"Wow! That's interesting. You mean to tell me there are hours of stored light and warmth in the candle, and we can't get at it because there is no wick? Is that what you are telling me?"

"Yes," says the puzzled woman.

"That's amazing, truly amazing," I say. "Why don't the two of you sit down, and let's talk about this." The two volunteers are applauded, and the talk continues.

I tell the congregation that this demonstration illustrates a dilemma. All we need to live purposeful, Spirit-filled lives is available to us, but we don't know how to access it. The candle exists, but it has no wick, and a wick is needed.

What is the wick that allows us to experience the light and warmth, the love and wisdom awaiting us? The answer: the wick is a person, but not just anybody. This wick is a person who is in a state of conscious oneness with the First Light; the wick is a person who is spiritually awake. Such an individual becomes an avenue for light and love and much more; this person assumes the mantle of the "light of the world" and is the wick in God's candle.

Jesus the Wick

Mark 5:22-43 is evidence that Jesus was a wick in God's candle. Jarius, one of the rulers of a synagogue, asked Jesus to come and heal his ill daughter. Jesus went with the father, and a multitude of people followed him. In the crowd was a woman who had suffered a flow of blood for twelve years. She thought that if she only touched the hem of Jesus' garment, she would be healed. Undoubtedly with great effort, she moved through the crowd, eventually touched Jesus' clothes—and was healed. Jesus knew something had happened and stopped and asked, "Who touched Me?" (Notice that Jesus did not say who touched my garment. He asked who touched Him.)

The woman did not simply touch the hem of Jesus' garment; she touched His consciousness. That consciousness was a wick in God's candle. In Jesus' awareness there was no flow of blood. In fact, Jesus knew nothing of the woman, and I also do not believe He was thinking about the sick child He was traveling to see. (The girl was dead when Jesus arrived at her home.) The wick Jesus embodied, the consciousness of His being, contained no death, no disease, only life and wholeness, and when the woman touched this consciousness, she was healed. In addition, Jarius' daughter, who had died, was restored to life. This is a story of spiritual consciousness at work. A pebble dropped in the pond and lives changed.

Dear friends, we are to be wicks in the candle. We are to walk the earth awake and aware of the truth and the nature of consciousness. In this way, we serve one another. Being spiritually awake does not make us powerful; it does not make us kings and queens; it makes us servants of one another. A wick is not the power; it is an avenue for the expression of power, wisdom, strength, love, peace, and joy.

God Does Not Fulfill Needs

The human experience is filled with challenge. We have needs, and we think God fulfills needs, but this is not true; however, needs serve a purpose, and they can be fulfilled. Needs can turn us to God, and this turn makes all the difference. In fact, when a need becomes evident in my life, and I remember its purpose, I let it turn me to the First Light.

This turn is important because one of the great spiritual breakthroughs occurs when we realize God does not fulfill needs. If God fulfilled needs, as soon as a need arose, it would be met, for as Joel Goldsmith said, "What God can do, God is doing."

God is not reluctant or slothful. God is not lazy; God is simply doing what God can do. And what is God doing? The experience at the burning bush taught us that God is "being." Consciousness is being our source, being love, being wisdom, being strength and much more.

The real question is: what are *we* doing? Most of the time, we are begging, beseeching, or affirming that our need is met. Our focus is the need. Our attention is on what is missing, what we lack. The focus on the need plants a seed that obeys the law, like begets like, and the need becomes our obsession. Lack produces lack.

There is a better way; let us become wicks in the candle.

Consciousness is like a wick. If the wick is filled with fear and thoughts of lack, we radiate darkness; but if the consciousness is that of the First Light, an avenue opens that allows the expression of the supply, wisdom, love, peace and strength that are available to us.

God does not fulfill needs. Fulfilling needs is not what God does, but needs can be met. First, we must know how the universe works. We are not recipients of creation; we are *participants* in creation. We do not exist in creation; creation emerges from within us. Our place is not on the circumference of the circle of creation. Our place is the center.

This is the divine dilemma; people are starving, people are in need and the storehouse is full, its doors open to us. We hold in our hands the candle with its capacity of heat and light, love and wisdom, but a wick is needed. We were created to be the wick of the candle. Without the wick, the candle does not burn, there is no light; there is no warmth.

This is our role in the creative process—we are destined to be the wick. In this way, we are avenues for expressions for all that the Creator is. We are here not simply to awaken; we are to be individualized expressions of the First Light. This brings us to the question: how do we become wicks in the candle, so the light can shine?

On Being A Wick In God's Candle

It is said that physical healing is humanity's greatest challenge. There are more prayers for healing than for any other human condition. Healing is possible because innately we are whole. How spiritual healing takes place, we do not fully understand, but we know it happens. This is true of the many human challenges we encounter.

Yet not all states of consciousness support healing. Some attitudes, beliefs, and behaviors make things worse. However, the good news is that there are states of mind that allow the light to shine.

Jesus said we are created to be "lights of the world," but how can the light shine unless there is a wick? For this, we were created. The First Light shone long ago. The birth of consciousness is recorded with these words: "Let there be light." All things are possible, the tallow of the candle is still warm. All it needs is a wick.

More provisions for the journey....

1. Awe, wonder, and curiosity take us deeper into the kingdom of heaven.
2. All that is needed is available.
3. "What God can do, God is doing." God does not fulfill needs, but human needs can be met. Needs turn us to God.
4. The question is: what are we doing?
5. Every candle needs a wick.
6. The wick in God's candle is a human being who is aware, spiritually awake.
7. We are not powerful; we are created to be avenues of divine power.
8. Consciousness is like a wick in a candle.

Come with me, and we will discover the power that changes lives and creates religions—the power of revelation.

Note: I wrote a book entitled, *How To Be A Wick In God's Candle.* The book was written for the prayer ministry of Unity of Fort Myers, Florida, the last ministry I served before retiring. It details how to become a wick in God's candle and how to build and develop a powerful and helpful prayer ministry.

CHAPTER ELEVEN

A More Recent Revelation

My Writing Career

My writing career began with poetry. It started long before anything was published in a magazine, an anthology of poetry, or as a book. I wrote poetry to girls I dated. I suspect the poetry wasn't very good because the girls seemed to lose interest in me once I dedicated a poem to them. Thank God I waited to write a poem to Nancy until after we were married.

The words to Nancy's poem started flowing through me as I drove to a hospital visitation in Raleigh, North Carolina. I scribbled the words on a notepad as I drove. "To My Wife On Christmas Day" became a Christmas gift to Nancy. Later the title of the poem was changed to "To A Friend" and was published in *Unity Magazine*. It became a greeting card, and I often read the poem when I officiated at weddings. My hope was that the couple become great friends who thought of one another with the same sentiment expressed in the poem. Here are the words of the poem I gave to Nancy on Christmas Day many years ago. It is the way I feel about her today. Actually, the essence of the words is more true today than when I scribbled them on a notepad on the way to the hospital.

To A Friend

There was a time when I thought
　　God walked beside you,
But now I see God moves
　　with every step you take.
There was a time when I thought
　　God loved you,
But now I feel you are the love
　　I often speak of.
There was a time when I thought
　　God had blessed you,
But now I know you
　　are His blessing for me.

I met Nancy in church. A folk singer, John Bassette, was sharing a sermon in song at her church, the United Church of Christ. I had dated Liz the night before, and we decided to meet at the church to hear John Bassette who had performed at Carnegie Hall in New York City. Liz was late, and I sat next to an attractive young woman with long blonde hair. We shared a hymnal, and as we sang, a man in the choir stared at me. (He was Nancy's father.) After the service, Nancy asked me if I wanted a tour of her church. What guy wants a tour of a church? Not me, but I was willing to spend more time with the attractive blonde with the long hair.

We toured the church and were together for the afternoon with another couple. It was the beginning of a life-long friendship and spiritual relationship that continues to deepen and grow. When a couple is first married, it can seem like the summit of love and oneness. Desires and feelings, like mist in a valley, obscure the heights of love that are possible. Nancy and I now live at a perpetual height of love and oneness that is evident as attraction, adoration, acceptance, and respect.

Apparently, people can sense what we have, and many have asked us to conduct marriage workshops to help others experience the same oneness. We always declined.

When Jamie, our oldest son, was engaged, he and Sara asked me to conduct their marriage ceremony. What an honor. However, Jamie became concerned because I told him that I was going to share some personal remarks about marriage with him, Sara, his friends, family, and all those in attendance. The night before the wedding Jamie and his brother Ben speculated about what I might say. They were concerned because Nancy and I have a reputation for outlandish remarks.

The time came during the ceremony when I said I had some personal remarks to share with Jamie and Sara about marriage. I pointed out the many years Nancy and I were married and that we had a powerful relationship. Then I said, "Here it is my advice—figure it out for yourself."

This is why we have never conducted marriage workshops. Each couple is unique, and each couple must figure it out for themselves.

"To A Friend" reveals much of how I feel about Nancy and what I believe about her essence, but I can assure you that the true feelings and beliefs cannot be expressed. I summarize our fifty-plus years of marriage like a newlywed—it has only just begun.

My first published work was a poem entitled, "Oneness." It appeared in the September 1975 issue of *Unity Magazine*. As I reflect on my life today, I see that this poem was the intersection of an event and an intuition that combined to become the foundation of my spiritual life.

On August 25, 1972 while I was in the Navy flying combat missions over North Vietnam, Nancy was in labor giving birth to our first son, James Jonathan Rosemergy, Jamie. She held a picture of me and wanted me to know that the child was being born. I was thousands of miles away in the Gulf of Tonkin on the aircraft carrier USS Kitty Hawk. I had stomach cramps, and the amazing thing was that I understood their meaning. I knew the child was being born.

I immediately wrote a note to Nancy and put it in the mail. Some hours later a message arrived telling me of the birth of our son and that both Nancy and Jamie were well. Commander Art Skelley, the commanding officer of the squadron RVAH-7, told me the news and asked if I had flown my mission for the day. I said I had. He replied, "Take the rest of the day off." I did.

I was a father. Since the cruise was more than ten months long and the build-ups to the cruise were months as well, Jamie was several months old when I saw him for the first time. I arrived home in the middle of the night, and Nancy took me into his room. Even now I can feel the emotion of gazing at our son for the first time. The light in the room was soft. He slept in peace, and I was thrilled.

The cramps told me of the coming birth, but they also declared a principle that is the foundation of my life—oneness. I did not consider the cramps to be evidence of this great spiritual truth when they occurred, but later they became a revelation that all are one, that miles and even time do not exist in the realms of Spirit and consciousness. Nancy wanted me to know of Jamie's birth, and her yearning was experienced by me in a way that I understood. This is one form of revelation, but there are many. In truth, this book is a record of one revelation after another, and so is this poem, "Oneness."

Oneness

When I hear the howl of the wind
    and that "still small voice"
    and know they are uttered
    by the same power,
The Father and I are one.
When the energy of a storm
    rages within me
    as zeal and zest for life

I have the power
to become what I am.
When I watch my son become a man
and a seed become a tree
and know they meet
at the crossroads called life,
The Father and I are one.
When I observe the order
of the heavens,
and the irresistible force of love
moves through my life,
the harmony of the universe is mine.
When I feel a gentle breeze
against my face,
and the loving squeeze of my love's hand
and know they stem from the same heart,
The Father and I are one.
When Christ, my "hope of glory,"
can be seen within me
and in my life,
I am what I am.
When the sunrise and the sunset
each marks a new beginning
for my eternal life,
The Father and I are one.

The basis of "Oneness" is Jesus' statement, "I and the Father are one." Its message can come as cramps during the birth of a child or the squeeze of Nancy's hand. This is the oneness of human things, but I am one with the God Jesus called Father. I now know the First Light to be consciousness itself. Every time I write or speak of consciousness, God whispers, "I am that I am."

I am as close to the Creator as I will ever be. Oneness is a state of being, but the question is whether I am conscious of the oneness.

This realization comes through revelation, spiritual breakthroughs that give no credence to creeds or dogma. Revelation transcends religion. There are ramifications if we honor the revelations that are contrary to long-held religious beliefs, but I am willing to pay the price even if I am called a heretic.

A Recent Revelation

My first book, *A Recent Revelation*, first appeared as a series of ten articles in *Unity Magazine*. They were controversial. The articles covered a variety of subjects ranging from "The Law of Creation" to "Prayer" to "The Devil" and "Death." Each article had two sections. The first section was written as if Jesus were speaking to humanity and providing new insights on the subject. The second section was the impact of these new insights on my life. The heresy was that I was putting words in Jesus' mouth. *Unity Magazine* received more mail about this series of articles than just about any series every printed in the magazine.

The editor, Tom Witherspoon, asked if I could write four additional "chapters," so the series could become a book. I added four additional subjects, and in 1981 *A Recent Revelation* was published. Everything I have written since is a *more recent revelation*. In fact, the idea of revelation or spiritual breakthrough is the heart of my spiritual journey.

I read extensively, scripture and the books, letters, essays, and talk transcripts of the most illumined people who have ever lived, but what has stirred me the most and become most relevant are my breakthroughs, revelations, and spiritual experiences. Such revelations are the cornerstones of religions and individual lives.

The Rock

Jesus gathered with His disciples at Caesarea Philippi in northern Israel. It was the location of one of the sources of the river Jordan and a seat of Roman power. A temple stood in front of a cave where a spring emerged from underground.

It was in this location at the foot of a cliff that Jesus asked His disciples, "Who do men say that I, the Son of Man, am?" (Matthew 16:13).

They answered, "Some say, John the Baptist, some Elijah, and others Jeremiah or one of the prophets" (Matthew 16:14).

He said to them, "But who do you say that I am?" (Matthew 16:15).

Simon Peter answered and said, "You are the Christ, the Son of the living God" (Matthew 16:16). It is interesting that Jesus was called a son of God in the shadow of a Roman temple where priests believed the Roman Emperor was a god.

Something astounding had happened, and Jesus recognized it. "Blessed are you, Simon Bar Jonah (Simon, son of Jonah), for flesh and blood has not revealed this to you, but My Father who is in heaven" (Matthew 16:17). In other words, Simon Peter experienced a revelation. The insight into Jesus' nature did not come from other people, but directly from The First Light. Jesus continued with one of the most misunderstood verses in the Bible. "And I also say to you that you are Peter, and on this rock I will build My church…" (Matthew 16:18).

This verse is interpreted to mean that Peter would become the rock or foundation of Jesus' church. Our Catholic friends established a long line of papal succession originating with the man Peter; however, I do not believe this was Jesus' intent. The rock upon which a church is established is the same foundation as a spiritual life—revelation.

The rock or foundation was not a man; it was not Peter. It was not Jesus. It is what happened to Simon Peter; he had a revelation; he had a spiritual experience. Revelation is the foundation of a spiritual life, a life that is destined to be a continuous stream of discoveries or spiritual breakthroughs. Every religion that is worth its salt began with a revelation. My way of life, Unity, began with Myrtle Fillmore's revelation that she was a child of God and therefore did not inherit sickness. Buddhism began with Siddhartha's revelation under the Bodhi tree. Islam began in a cave when Mohammed experienced the "night of power." The beginning of every religion is revelation, an experience of the consciousness of Being—*I am that I am*. The bush burns once again without being consumed. The beginning of our spiritual lives is always a revelation, and revelation continues as a sustaining breath for all who live a spiritual life. Because revelation is the beginning of every religion and at the heart of our spiritual lives and human experience, it tends to create heresy. Religious leaders often attempt to preserve the core beliefs of their religion by insisting that the typical person is unable to receive revelations. Revelation is reserved for a worthy few. This is not true.

Revelation is the driving force, validity, and relevance of our spiritual lives. Every individual is called to revelation and awakening. These spiritual experiences and insights are often labeled heretical, and they are often dismissed, but they should be examined, for revelation is what changes and validates religions and lives. Wonder, curiosity, awe and desire may be the first touch of the Divine, but revelation is the continuing embrace.

Most religions promise salvation from a future hell, but the gift of a spiritual way of life is daily revelation. We saw this in Jesus' encounter with Nicodemus. A second birth, spiritual birth, opens our eyes so we can see the kingdom of God that is at hand. This is the future of spirituality. Religions will once again become relevant and a part of daily life when they serve as midwives for the birth that awaits us. The promise is not salvation; it is conscious oneness with the First Light. It comes to us not when we die, but when we are born anew.

A Blinding Revelation

Not all revelations are gentle; some are jarring, some are blinding. Remember, Saul experienced this kind of revelation on the road to Damascus.

> *...suddenly a light shone around him...he fell to the ground, and heard a voice saying to him, "Saul, Saul, why do you persecute Me?" And he said, "Who are You, Lord?" Then the Lord said, "I am Jesus, whom you are persecuting."*
>
> Acts 9:3-5

The light of revelation can be blinding. This is particularly true when our personal identity or ego is immense. Truth blinds us. It is like emerging from the darkness of a cave and standing in the light. We cannot see. The nothingness of darkness can obscure our vision, but the somethingness of light and truth can overwhelm us.

A More Recent Revelation

Little did I know when I wrote *A Recent Revelation* that the experience of the First Light would be a foundational principle of my life. All breakthroughs come in this way. Einstein's insights were a revelation to him and the world. The forward march of human knowledge and insight, whether of the cosmos or the kingdom of heaven, comes through revelation.

In the 1990's I was invited to speak at Unity of Columbia, Missouri, on the subject of conflict and peace. I received the invitation because I was a nexus, an intersection, of war and peace. I was a Vietnam veteran and a minister. I shared my lecture and shortly thereafter was invited to be a part of a peace-studies group at the University of Missouri. One evening I was one of three members of a panel presenting ideas on peace in a public forum.

I chose to talk about a verse of scripture that was a source of division and conflict between religions and to introduce the heretical idea that this statement that sowed division was actually a verse validating the many religions of the world.

Here is Jesus' statement.

> *"I am the way, the truth and the life. No one comes to the Father except through Me."*
>
> John 14: 6

This statement has been used to drive a wedge between religions and to diminish spiritual disciplines other than Christianity. It seems to say that Jesus is the only way to God. However, revelation sheds new light on the verse and validates other paths to the Creator. It is simple logic.

Jesus defined Himself as A=B. Jesus=the way, the truth and the life. Those who come to God must come through Him, through the way, truth, and the life. No religion is the sole proprietor of truth. In fact, truth is a personal experience. It is not real for us; it does not enable us to find our way or live the life unless we know the truth through experience. For instance, we can study the laws of aerodynamics and hear people tell tales of flying in an aircraft, but we don't actually know what it is to fly until the airplane is airborne, and we look out of the cockpit window.

Here is another relevant Jesus statement, "...know the truth, and the truth shall make you free" (John 8:32). This knowing is not intellectual; it is life-transforming and can be earth shattering, a metaphysical earthquake in which things are not falling apart; they are falling together. Saul's preconceived opinion about the followers of the Way crumbled on the road to Damascus, and I, too, have felt the ground move under my feet.

This interpretation of Jesus' famous "I am the way" statement validates all religions and paths to God. The prerequisite is not an allegiance to Jesus, but to knowing the truth. This is the way, and it enables us to live the life.

After my presentation, there was a lively discussion of all the ideas shared that evening. I sensed there was relief on the part of the public that the journey to God was not a particular religion, but that the way was truth and life. Sometimes the great things of life need to be reduced to their simplest form: know the truth and live according. This is the way.

The Early Days

In 1975, Thelma Hembroff, a fellow student of the Unity School for Religious Studies, invited me into a life of revelation. She asked if I would pray with her before class each morning. We sat together in silence in a small space adjoining our classrooms. I had no idea what I was doing. Remember, I entered ministerial school having attended only a half a dozen Unity church services.

Eventually, my focus became Jesus' simplest prayer: *I and the Father are one.* I realized that most of humanity, myself included, prayed about many things. Jesus primarily prayed about one thing: conscious oneness with His Father. His prayer was *I and the Father are one.* My prayer became: The Father and I are one. It was the best beginning for someone new to Unity and to the contemplative life. It was one of my first revelations.

My studies at Unity Village were a call for revelation. Because I was so new to Unity, everything was new to me. I read the writings of Unity authors, but I longed for a personal experience of the ideas I read about and learned about in class. I wanted my own definitions, my own understanding of the wonderful concepts I was discovering. I yearned for discovery, and through Thelma's invitation, I learned that revelation's classroom was silence.

Another classmate, Ross Tucker, watered the seed planted by Thelma. Ross was in the class behind mine. Prior to our graduation,

Ross and each member of his class, the class of 1977, selected a verse of scripture to give to each graduating member of my class, the class of 1976. Ross gave me the following scripture, "And I looked, and behold, a white horse. He who sat on it had a bow; and a crown was given to him, and he went out conquering and to conquer" (Revelation 6:2). Quite a verse, isn't it? It called for revelation. Eventually, years later, I realized the rider represented spiritual awakening. My purpose as a minister came into focus. Printed on the back of some of my books is this revelation—that I am to serve as a midwife for the spiritual awakening of the human family.

Long ago, this gift of scripture from Ross Tucker declared my life's work. Ministers have many roles, but I discovered that I ride a white horse and carry a bow. May the arrows I sling pierce the heart and reveal what is most important—conscious oneness with the One.

The revelations of others are important. They stimulate our minds, but truth is not of the intellect; it is an experience to be put to the test. Revelations and insights become dear friends that support a contemplative life, but "daily bread" is required, new insights and revelations. Remember we are always half way there—the journey is infinite; the cosmos is vast, and the kingdom is at hand waiting to be discovered.

The Promise

Revelations were joy, bundles of energy and light. They called to me, and they often confused me. It was as though I was tied to the mast of a ship hearing and being taunted by the siren's call. I was married, a father, the minister of Unity of Raleigh, North Carolina, but I was tormented. I did not know how to balance the call of silence and the work of daily living. It appeared that I knew my way, but I did not. The confusion lasted for years.

One day while we lived in Raleigh, I took Nancy for a walk at a neighborhood park and told her that I was considering leaving the ministry, not just Unity of Raleigh, but ministry itself. I told her I was living between two worlds. It was gutting my soul. I didn't know how to live this way.

For years this was my life. Eventually, I became the minister of Unity Church of Truth in Spokane, Washington. I was the reluctant minister. My contract with the church provided me three days a quarter for personal reflection and prayer and meditation. During these times, I was alone. I took my own food and ate alone. I took no books to read, just a pen and steno pad. Usually, I was in the woods in a cabin on a lake or in the mountains. These times fed my soul. Ideas came, and they helped the church. Revelations continued, but unrest still dominated my soul.

I suspected I had the answer, the key, but had not yet learned how to turn the key and create a life that balanced daily living and being a monk of the city.

Finally, I saw, I really saw the promise.

> *"...do not worry, saying, 'What shall we eat?' or 'What shall we drink?' or 'What shall we wear?' For after all these things the Gentiles seek. For your heavenly Father knows that you need all these things. But seek first the kingdom of God and His righteousness, and all these things shall be added to you."*
>
> Matthew 6:31-33

There it was—the promise. My focus was on what I thought were two paths, a spiritual path and the path of daily living. I was wrong. There was only one path, the spiritual path, and if I pursued it and lived it, all else would be added to me. I swung my attention from the contemplative life to the human experience, trying to divide my time between the two. The promise revealed a simple life—God first and all else follows. Seek the kingdom, whatever it is, and those things I had given so much time to would be added to me without them being a focus of my life. No more divided attention.

The Pony

While ministering in Spokane, I jogged. My route took me past a pasture where a pony lived. During the autumn as the winter approached, I noticed the pony's fur thickening. One day, I stopped to talk to him.

I said, "Where did you get that coat? At a department store, some consignment store, at Goodwill?"

The pony replied, "It came from within."

Strange, but I never saw the pony straining to grow the coat. It was natural. It was added to him.

The pony tilted his head to the side, smiled, and said, "Manifestation is none of my business."

My jog continued. I had met a master, a pony who revealed a more recent revelation. If I seek the kingdom, I don't need to give undue attention to manifestation or what Jesus called "added things." There was a way to face the challenges of daily living through seeking the kingdom. I was hopeful, but a question remained. What was the kingdom?

More provisions for the journey….

1. Oneness, a conscious awareness of the First Light, is a foundational principle of a spiritual life.
2. Revelation is a foundational principle of a spiritual life.
3. Jesus' way of life is oneness, His prayer is, "I and the Father are one." His prayer became my prayer, too.
4. Revelation revealed that the foundation of a spiritual life is spiritual birth or awakening.
5. Jesus revealed that the way to God is truth, and that life is the living of the truth.
6. We cannot live between two worlds because there is only one world.
7. Here is the promise: seek first the kingdom (whatever it is) and all else will be added. This is my "business."

Come with me as we discover the kingdom of God, the kingdom of heaven. I cannot tell you everything I uncovered, but I can tell you enough so that you, too, will seek the kingdom above all else, so that life that seems so complex can become simple. I promise you will not fear the dark. You will see darkness as mystery and know it is the place where faith is born. You will come to know that faith is not a place of knowing; it is a place of doubt and darkness, a placed where the tiniest light can illumine the way.

CHAPTER TWELVE

Hidden In Plain Sight

A Complication

I saw the promise, "...seek first the kingdom...and these things shall be added to you," and I was willing to put it to the test. All earthly matters were reprioritized. Once they were paramount, all consuming, a focus of my life; now they were "added things." My understanding was that if I sought the kingdom (whatever it is), everything needed for earthly living would be added to me without making money, health, and career, etc. the main focus of my life. The promise was that my earthly life would flow from my spiritual life. The simplicity appealed to me. I loved the phrase, "added things." It seemed right, but there was a complication. I did not know what to seek.

Like much of humanity, I was taught and had come to believe that the kingdom of heaven or kingdom of God was the place where God lived. It was a location. After death, I might join God in this place—if I lived a good and moral life. This rudimentary understanding of heaven did not seem compatible with the promise. The church's promise was about tomorrow. Jesus' promise was about today. A search began. What is the kingdom? Perhaps Jesus hid the answer in plain sight, requiring an eye to see and an ear to hear.

What I discovered was stunning. Jesus' kingdom was not the kingdom of the church. The path to the kingdom was not death; it was life. The Master revealed the nature of the kingdom in more than thirty parables and multiple statements. His teachings were in plain sight, but obscured by a veil of religious dogma. In fact, a third of Jesus' ministry was about the kingdom. That's how important it is. After His temptations, Jesus began His three-year ministry by proclaiming that the kingdom everyone was waiting for was actually already here. "Repent, for the kingdom of heaven is at hand" (Matthew 4:17).

It's Here

Jesus asked the people to repent, to change their thinking about the kingdom of heaven. The Jews of Jesus' time longed for the coming of the messiah, the establishment of the kingdom and the dismantling of the pagan Roman Empire. Today, Christianity and other religions are longing for the establishment of a kingdom on earth. Jesus saw the kingdom, not by gazing into the future, but by close examination of the present moment.

The kingdom is at hand, in the grasp of the people. The kingdom is here. It is no wonder that Jesus said again and again, "He who has eyes to see, let him see."

Seeing, knowing and discovering the kingdom is a matter of consciousness. It is here, but we must have eyes to see—our consciousness must become an eye that can comprehend the kingdom—whatever it is.

Like A Child

Jesus reinforced the idea of a present kingdom on several occasions. One day, people brought their children to Jesus, so He could bless them. His disciples tried to deny this, but Jesus said, "Let the little children come to Me, and do not forbid them; for such is the kingdom of heaven" (Matthew 19:14). Apparently, there are qualities children possess that enable them to possess the kingdom. I believe the qualities are awe, wonder, and curiosity. We explored these qualities earlier and found them to be evidence of the presence of God. These signs are particularly strong in children; however, they also are present in adults even though logic and hurtful experiences may shield us from the joy of discovery and from being fully alive.

One day when I was minister of Unity Temple on the Plaza in Kansas City, Ben, our younger son, stared out a picture window in our home as his older brother, Jamie, approached. Jamie asked, "What are you looking for?"

Ben replied, "Eternal life." Indeed, the spiritual quest is strong in the youngest of us.

I remember when Nancy and I set up our eight-inch telescope one clear night on the fourth fairway of the golf course at Unity Village and started visually roaming from one bright object in the night sky to another. Suddenly, I saw it hanging in the sky—Saturn with its majestic rings. I can't imagine anyone seeing this planet and its rings for the first time without gasping for breath. Nancy looked into the eyepiece and became a child again. Awe and wonder are always close at hand.

Born Again

We can change our thinking and discover the kingdom is at hand. We can adopt the qualities of a child and see what others fail to see. And we can be born again.

Remember the Jesus' dialogue with his night visitor, Nicodemus, a member of the Sanhedrin, the ruling religious body of Israel. This clandestine meeting reinforced the truth that the kingdom of God is here and that our consciousness determines whether we see it or not. Jesus' message to Nicodemus and to us is that we must be born again or awaken spiritually before we can see the kingdom. Human thinking, dogmas, and creeds are not enough. There is a spiritual kingdom to discover, and it requires a spiritual birth to see it.

Nicodemus wanted to know if Jesus was the messiah, the herald of what was to come. Jesus was the messiah, but not a prophet who ushered in the kingdom. He was a visionary who came to remove the blinders from the eyes of the people, so they could see what was hidden in plain sight.

These events in Jesus' life inform us about the kingdom of God and how to experience it. None of these events tells us what the kingdom is, but we are learning that what we seek is in plain sight. Scales are falling from our eyes. We see dimly, but we are beginning to understand.

Such insights fanned the flame of my desire to study Jesus' parables about the kingdom and to explore His statements about the elusive treasure I sought. This study led me to the riddle.

The Riddle

I love a riddle, but some riddles take years to solve. How do I unravel this mystery of all mysteries? What is the kingdom? First, I had to let go of preconceived ideas about the kingdom, for the greatest impediment to truth is often what is believed to be true, but is not.

It got confusing. Jesus said the kingdom is here, but He, also, said it is coming. How can something be here and be coming at the same time?

The confusion increased when I read these words, "Now when He was asked by the Pharisees when the kingdom of God would come, 'He answered them and said, "The kingdom of God does not come with observation; or will they say, 'See here!' or 'See there!' For indeed, the kingdom of God is within you" (Luke 17:20-21).

Remember in chapter two when we stood in the Hebrew camp and saw the Tabernacle in the midst of the people? Perhaps it was this image Jesus held in mind when He said that the kingdom is within us; it is in the midst of each individual like the Tabernacle is in the middle of the Hebrew encampment.

I was confused, but I was gathering insight. The kingdom is here, it is coming and it is within me. At least I have a place to look—my own consciousness—for it is not observed in the world. Wow! Confusion continued, but perhaps it is the mother of wisdom.

The Parables

I turned to the parables to try to solve the riddle, "What is the kingdom of God like? And to what shall I compare it?"

"It is like a mustard seed, which a man took and put in his garden; and it grew and became a large tree, and the birds of the air nested in its branches" (Luke 13:18-19).

The kingdom is like a seed; it grows until it supports even more growth. The pieces are coming together. The kingdom is here; it is coming, it is within us, and it grows. And there is more.

And again He said, "To what shall I liken the kingdom of God?

"It is like leaven, which a woman took and hid in three measures of meal until it was all leavened" (Luke 13:20-21). It spreads until it permeates my entire being.

"Again, the kingdom of heaven is like treasure hidden in a field, which a man found and hid; and for joy over it he goes and sells all that he has and buys that field.

"Again, the kingdom of heaven is like a merchant seeking beautiful pearls, who when he had found one pearl of great price, went and sold all that he had and bought it" (Matthew 13:44-45).

The kingdom, whatever it is, is the most precious thing in my life. I will sell everything in order to have it.

I am beginning to see. The kingdom is here; it is coming; it is within me, it grows, it spreads, and it is the most precious thing in my life. I must seek it. And there is more...much more.

"Again, the kingdom of heaven is like a dragnet that was cast into the sea and gathered some of every kind, which, when it was full, they drew to shore; and they sat down and gathered the good into vessels, and threw the bad away" (Matthew 13:47-48).

Apparently, there is a sorting process associated with the kingdom. There are things to retain, and things to discard.

There are more parables explaining various qualities and aspects of the kingdom, but it would be too cumbersome for us to explore all of them. Perhaps that is the subject of another book. However, we have enough to solve the riddle. We know the qualities. It is here, it is coming, it is within us, it grows, it spreads, it is the most valuable thing in our lives, and there is a sorting process associated with it. And finally, just by seeking the kingdom all those things I once considered vitally important are added unto me. I don't need to make them the object of my life. The question is: what one thing has all these qualities?

The Riddle Solved

I concluded that the kingdom is consciousness, a specific consciousness—an awareness of our oneness with the First Light and all creation. This consciousness is here waiting for us to experience it. In fact, each of us has at least a rudimentary understanding of the First Light. We are curious, and from time to time we are filled with awe and wonder. We are filled with desires, and in their pure form they transcend our base human needs, but regardless of our current awareness of our oneness, more is coming. The depth of the connection and oneness we share is infinite. There is a burning bush to see and subtle colors of the rainbow to discover. We may experience a thread of oneness with our beloved, but a bond of unity is present with all people and all creation. There are living creatures, plants and animals, but even the rocks breathe.

Each realization of such things is the seed growing into a state of mind that supports more growth and casts more seed. This consciousness begins small, like a pinch of leaven in a measure of flour, but it spreads. We may feel our oneness with our source and experience security, but we may be unaware that there is a bond we share with all people. We are prosperous, but we have few friends. We may be loving and kind, but our bodies are weak and sickly. In one area of life our consciousness is strong, but in another dimension of life, there is much to discover.

This consciousness is the treasure, the pearl of great price. Without it, we know little, but as it grows and we learn what aspect of mind and heart to retain and what must be discarded, we become increasingly aware and recognize our quest is to be conscious. Just as the First Light is filled with curiosity and wonder and probes the universe in ways we do not know, so too, do we explore through living our lives, giving allegiance to the silence and forgetting self. The universe is vast and space expands at relativistic speeds, but our consciousness has no horizons. It has no need of speed because it has nowhere to go; it is everywhere; it is now here.

I solved the riddle. The kingdom is an ever-expanding cosmic consciousness experienced through spiritual birth and revelation. It grows like a seed and spreads like leaven in and through my consciousness, but is it relevant to my daily life? I discovered that it is.

The Kingdom Comes Alive

My father was in the Coast Guard, and we moved frequently. One year I was in three different schools. On Ocracoke Island on the Outer Banks of North Carolina where my mother was raised, I attended a one-room school where each row of desks was a different grade. One teacher taught us all. As I grew older, moving became more difficult. Leaving friends was anguish. During one move I had to leave my first girlfriend. I refused to speak to my parents for three days. Not a word.

When I was a senior at West Jefferson High School on the west bank of the Mississippi River near New Orleans, my parents planned to move again. I was deeply entrenched with friends and with my high-school tennis team. I refused to go with my parents, so they arranged for me to stay with longtime family friends. At age seventeen, I was supervised, but on my own. I became more and more independent, confident, and self-assured, but at first it was anguish being away from my family. I remember entering the house where I stayed my senior year, going into my room, lying on the bed and quietly crying.

Life progressed from high school to college, to the Navy, to marriage, to fatherhood, to ministerial school, to ordination, to pioneering a ministry in Raleigh, North Carolina. I was confident, probably too confident, whole and filled with energy, but there was an area of my life where the First Light did not shine—prosperity. My first salary at Unity of Raleigh was $800 a month, and yet we owned a house and two cars. I remember listening to a television program and learning that we lived below the poverty level. Our income grew, but money is not a true indicator of well-being and security, because I still felt lack. I had a simple dream to be able to take Nancy and our two sons to a restaurant once a week.

I did not realize it at the time, but there was a need for the leaven, a consciousness of the First Light, to spread into this area of my life, and for seeds to grow and support even more spiritual growth, revelation, and insight. I thought the answer was money. It took years before I realized the solution was a series of spiritual breakthroughs.

As I review my life, I realize that seeds were planted and growing. Unconscious growth was occurring. Seeds were planted, but I don't remember placing them in the ground, the fields of my mind, and caring for them.

While in ministerial school, I worked as a teaching tennis pro at Woodside Racquet Club in Kansas City. During that time, we received a tax bill of one hundred and eight dollars. We did not have the money to pay it. One night in prayer and meditation an idea came to me: sell your hand gun. My father gave me this gun, a 9 mm Walther. I purchased hollow point rounds for the clip that held 15 bullets. Nancy hated the gun. On Wednesday, my day off from teaching tennis and after ministerial classes, I told Nancy I had an errand to run. I drove to a gun shop in Raytown, Missouri and sold the weapon and the rounds. Interesting...I received exactly one hundred and eight dollars for the gun and bullets. I returned home and told Nancy about my prayer time and the sale of the gun. For us, it was a miracle and evidence that seeds were growing; a needed consciousness was spreading in me and through the family. I was born anew; revelations and insights fed us, literally.

Like those who cast their dragnet into the sea and tossed their catch on the shore, I sorted fish as well. There is no better place to experience the parables and statements Jesus made about the kingdom of heaven then in ministry.

There was great growth taking place in my first ministry at Unity of Raleigh in North Carolina. Great relationships were forming with the people. In the first months of ministry, I found what every minister is destined to find—Almitra.

My Almitra is named Mary Mooney. Forty-five years after our first meeting, we remain dear friends. The name Almitra comes from Kahlil Gibran's poetic masterpiece, *The Prophet*. In this book, the prophet speaks to the people, but he is introduced each time by

Almitra who was the first person to have faith in the prophet and to support him and his ministry.

Mary Mooney was the first person to exhibit faith in me as a minister. She came to me for counseling, and we have walked the spiritual path with one another ever since. Although we have lived hundreds and thousands of miles from one another, our paths touch from time to time, and each encounter is a blessing to me. I cherish my Almitra.

Unity Church of Raleigh was a pioneer ministry that began with a study group of 18 people. In two years, we were looking for a church home. We found a suitable building with an adjacent house at 805 Glenwood Ave. We needed $25,000 for a down payment. On the weekend before we were to close on the property a snowstorm struck in Raleigh, and I cancelled church on the Sunday people were to bring their gifts for the down payment. Elliot Fisher, our treasurer, put chains on the tires of his car and went from home to home to pick up the needed gifts. We bought the church and made it our spiritual home. The adjoining house became a home for battered spouses. There were "added things," but I did not consciously understand the growth that was happening in me. The years progressed and the security seed and sense of well-bring grew with each revelation, and with each spiritual experience, I cast out erroneous beliefs and embraced the truth.

One belief cast aside concerned needs, the prevalent human hope and belief that God fulfills needs. Humanity has prayed this prayer for thousands of years. Sometimes it seems to work; at other times we wonder why it fails. We question our faith, and we question if God cares.

I discovered that God does not fulfill needs. This does not mean needs cannot be met, but it does demand that we know how the universe works, that we discover the universal laws that govern our lives. Basically, needs are not avenues for the expression of cosmic power or the Source. If needs were an avenue for God's expression as soon as a need arose, it would be met, for "what God can do, God is doing." This quote by Joel Goldsmith is brimming with truth. God is not lazy, slothful, or reluctant. God does not fulfill needs, but God is the Source, and if we can discover the avenue through which the Source flows into our lives, we find security and well-being.

We tend to dwell on our needs, but a need is like a seed, a seed whose harvest is more of the same—lack. I learned that the avenue through which the source flowed into my life was a consciousness of the First Light, an awareness of the source of all things. Needs can be an impediment to security if we dwell on what we lack, but needs do have a role to play in our lives. They turn us to the First Light, to the consciousness that is our Source.

The Way of Prosperity

In future chapters, we will explore the prayer and meditative practices at the heart of a spiritual life that bring security and well-being, but there are also actions we must take in our daily lives that support and deepen our understanding that a consciousness of God is our supply.

Most people think prosperity is a straight line. Something flows from a source to us. This is not true. This belief is another fish to cast aside. Prosperity is not a straight line; it is a circle that flows, and I am the one who must initiate the flow.

We tend to believe that we demonstrate prosperity when we acquire something, a sum of money, a healing or a new job, but this is not true. We demonstrate prosperity when we give and express.

Many times, I stood before a congregation and held up a fifty-dollar bill and asked, "Who deserves this fifty-dollar bill?" Most of the audience simply stares at me, but there are a few people who raise their hands, and the first person I notice receives the money. The person comes forward, and I ask if the fifty-dollar bill is authentic. The person says yes, and the money belongs to them. Then the fun begins, for there are many lessons in this illustration.

I ask the audience, "Why weren't all your hands up? Don't you deserve a fifty-dollar bill? How will you ever experience the riches of the kingdom of God if you don't feel you deserve fifty dollars?" This is usually a powerful realization for people.

I remember speaking at an Amway meeting in Spokane, Washington and holding up a twenty-dollar bill and asking who deserved it. No one raised his hand. Not one person. Finally, Nancy, my wife, who was with me, raised her hand, and I gave her the twenty dollars. Receptivity is a powerful lesson, particularly for those who want to prosper.

In a church setting when I give away fifty dollars, I ask an additional question of the audience. "Who demonstrated fifty dollars?" The conventional wisdom is that the person who received the money made the demonstration. I challenge this notion by saying that it is not the person who receives that demonstrates, but the person who gives.

Imagine what would happen to a society if it valued giving more than receiving. This is the kingdom of heaven growing and spreading and coming into being in a person's life. In this instance, I was the child learning the truth about prosperity, sorting out the many beliefs held by humanity and casting out error and embracing the truth.

I share these experiences because I want people to know the efficacy of the "seek first the kingdom" way of life. All things are added. The kingdom spreads in all areas of life, the consciousness of truth expands and grows, and life is a wonder. Here is one more example of a spiritual breakthrough in the area of life called prosperity.

Radical Generosity

When I served as the minister of Unity of Fort Myers, Florida, we grew in attendance and in consciousness until we needed a new 400-seat sanctuary. We retained an architect, a construction company, and a fund-raising company. Rev. Tom Melzoni guided us through the fund and consciousness raising processes that enabled us to build our sanctuary. We practiced "radical generosity."

Through radical generosity, we entered the circle of giving and found ourselves at our extremity. Nancy and I experienced this spiritual practice over many meetings and many months. We attended every congregational meeting where we and the congregation talked about what the spiritual community meant to us and about the different ways people could support the building and consciousness raising project. After each meeting I asked Nancy how much we were going to give. (We started with one number and over the months we increased our giving tenfold.) Here's what happened.

We kept raising the amount we were going to give until our ego pushed back. It said, "You can't do that. If you give that amount, you won't be able to retire and live as you want to live. If you give that amount, it will be your ruin." (Our egos were quite dramatic.) We raised the number until, we felt the push-back, and then we waited. Sometimes, we decided to give more, but there came a time when there was peace. Radical generosity took us to the limit of our consciousness, and then we took one more step and broke through into a new sense of security and well-being. It was a state of being marked by peace and a willingness to act.

Many members of the congregation discovered the power of radical generosity and its ability to break down barriers and bring a new understanding of prosperity. This was my journey, one that brought understanding and a new way of life. The result wasn't a prosperous life; the result was a generous life, and I am sure it never ends, for I am always half way there.

Conclusion

Jesus' way of life is now my way of being, not salvation and sacrifice, but awakening and revelation, a way of seeing and knowing the truth. All things are a part of me. I am a child of wonder, a newborn not learning to walk, but learning to see. I plant a seed and don't have to wait for the blossom and the fruit to form. The harvest has come. I can taste the sweet leaven in the bread I eat, and I am rich beyond compare, for I am awake and awakening. The consciousness of the First Light is more vast than the cosmos, and it is a part of me and everyone who is the light of the world. And to think—it was all hidden in plain sight.

More provisions for the journey….

1. The kingdom is hidden in plain sight.
2. It is here, it is coming, for there is always more to know and experience.
3. It is within us, growing and spreading.
4. It is the most valuable thing in our lives.
5. Within our consciousness, there is that which is retained, for it is truth, and there is error that must be tossed aside.
6. The kingdom is our conscious oneness with the ever-expanding consciousness God is.
7. We are in tune with the Infinite, for we are explorers aligned to the First Light seeking to become increasingly aware.

Come with me and I will tell you of another revelation that changed my life—the Sacred Human.

CHAPTER THIRTEEN

The Sacred Human

Father and Mother

My father meant well, but I often interpreted his words to be unaccepting. At times it was subtle and at other times it was not. I never consciously thought, "He doesn't love me or accept me as I am," but it was an unconscious conclusion I drew over the course of many years. If I received a "B" in a course, he asked where was the "A?" If I got an "A" on a paper, he wanted to know why it wasn't an "A+." This was the subtle message of nonacceptance. The overt messages usually came during our evening meal. This was the time of raving and ranting. This was when my father's suppressed rage asserted itself. I remember verbal attacks for not properly enunciating the word, "the." "Pass dah potatoes" got me in trouble. Needless to say, I ate my meal as fast as I could to get away from the table and his anger; however, anger was simmering in me, an anger that eventually asserted itself and threatened to rule my life.

My first response to his questions and anger was a pursuit of perfection, the elusive self-defeating quest leading to a false conclusion—I am not enough. I was not obsessed with getting his approval, but I was driven to excel. He also had a strong work ethic;

it blended well with the pursuit of perfection and had a constructive effect on me. When my father started a project and managed to finish it, it was done right. I channeled these influences, non-acceptance and the work ethic, in a positive direction, but eventually I discovered that what can be a positive influence in school, sports, and career can be a detriment to spiritual growth.

The pursuit of perfection spread throughout my life. As a Boy Scout, I became a Senior Patrol Leader. I played tennis and was the number one player and Most Valuable Player on my high school and college teams. I was a Distinguished Naval Graduate and received a regular commission in the United States Navy. (This enabled me to resign my commission before my contract ended, so I could enter ministerial school at Unity Village in Missouri). I was loved by most of the people in the churches I served, although there was always at least one person who echoed my father's questions that indicated I was not the person I needed to be.

My mother was quiet, supportive, and protective. We did things together. We were a team collecting pecans. I threw my football into the branches and knocked the nuts to the ground where she harvested them. We went to the drugstore for vanilla Cokes. We had so much fun together that I did not want to go to school and be away from her. First grade was miserable. She saw my anguish and worked in the school cafeteria in the elementary school in Great Bridge, Virginia near Norfolk. Imagine a child coming through the line in the cafeteria and having his plate prepared, including the meat cut in tiny bite-sized portions. In the afternoon she was a school bus monitor. Needless to say, I was a mama's boy. It was sports that enabled me to pull away from my mother and continue my journey into manhood.

The greatest blessing of my parents was that they were explorers. We were Methodist, but my folks explored spiritual things. When I was quite young, they gave me a copy of Thomas Sugrue's *There Is A River*, the story of Edgar Cayce's life. It opened my consciousness to a spirituality without bounds. It was the beginning of the journey beyond the god of dogma and creeds, to a God that is an ever-expanding consciousness.

Two Men

I was fortunate to have two men in my life who supported my desire for excellence, but who were also accepting of who I was and who I was becoming. The first was Dr. Winston Peter Riehl, my high-school tennis coach. When I met Doc Riehl, I was sixteen, and he was in his mid-thirties. He was cool. He smoked a pipe, drove a sports car and was calm, a sharp contrast to my father. He recognized my desire for excellence and worked with me on my tennis strokes and instructed me in how to win. He took me to other coaches for their comments on my game. I never took lessons, but I was exposed to gifted tennis instructors.

Doc Riehl made tennis exciting. I played in the Louisiana State championships after playing tennis for less than a year and traveled to Mexico to play against a local champion. He invited me to go to Camp Menatoma near Readsfield, Maine, to be a counselor and to teach tennis to the campers, rich kids from the northeastern United States. I taught tennis, coached the camp tennis team, and led mountain trips for five Maine summers.

My first year at Menatoma, we said I was 19 years old when I was only 17. We lied about my age because there were attendees older than I at the camp. I fell in love with Maine, at least Maine in the summer. During that time, I was runner-up in the boy's state tennis championship, and as a young adult I won the Central Maine State Open.

Doc's influence on my life was immense. He was an example of what a man could be. At the time, I did not grasp how important he was in my development and how timely his presence was in my life. He embodied peace. Doc was quick on a tennis court, but he moved deliberately and with calm assurance in life. I remember being at tennis practice with Doc and my fellow team members. The football team was practicing nearby. A football coach rushed over and asked Doc to come to the stadium because a player had broken his leg. Doc Riehl lit his pipe and calmly followed the coach to the injured boy.

In a strange way, my ministerial journey began that next day. I knew the injured boy. He and I ran in different crowds, but I remember having a great conversation with him in the gym one day. I made my first hospital visit to see him. He was surprised to see me, but I was glad to be with him. I don't ever remember talking with him again.

Here's what I learned: when the going gets tough, slow down and take a breath, because out of the peace can come right action and a positive outcome. This was helpful playing tennis, and it is certainly the thing to do when unexpected challenges bring us to our knees. As long as we are kneeling, we might as well feel the energy of the earth and the power of peace.

Another man, Ed Davenport, was an unparalleled and ongoing influence on my life. He is my best friend, and although Ed is in his nineties, we are as close as ever. I met Ed while serving as the minister in Raleigh. He saw a print advertisement that Unity of Raleigh placed in the newspaper and called our home. We had no church building at the time and counseling and classes took place in our tiny yellow house. I was not home and Nancy took the call. When I returned, she told me she had just talked to the nicest man.

Ed came to our home for counseling. We sat in my small office, and he told me about one of his daughters who was experiencing health challenges. She was currently in the hospital, and he asked if I would visit her. I did, and my friendship with Ed Davenport began.

I have more memories of Ed than I can relate, but I think I loved best our walks on the beach. We would walk for an hour or more and talk about spiritual growth, family, and truth ideas. I cherished our conversations. I remember that it was during one of those walks that I told Ed I considered him to be my best friend.

Ed is totally accepting. He is an explorer, a revolutionary who followed his own guidance. Ed is as independent a person as I know.

He loves people and although I count him as my best friend, I believe there are many people who think of Ed in this way. Gratitude and generosity flow from him like a mighty river. I don't think I have ever had a conversation with him when he did not express gratitude for life and the people in his life.

My friend Ed journals and writes essays and poetry, and his writings reveal the depth of his being. And there is a great humility about him. When I was the minister of Unity of Raleigh, I asked him to speak on Sunday when I was away, but he declined. Believe me, people would have loved his ideas, gentle spirit, and vision that sees what few can see.

Both Ed and Doc filled a void of constructive male influence in my life. My father was not able to do so and during much of my teenage years, I was not with my family. Doc was there, and when I started ministry and every year since, Ed was always near, just a phone call away.

Let's Try Maintenance

I had great role models; they supported me. I tried my best, I went the extra mile, and I excelled in my endeavors, but it was not enough. I believed I was not enough, so I tried another approach—suppression and blame. I pushed the feelings of inadequacy aside and when someone triggered the feelings, I turned from them. If I didn't have to deal with the person, maybe I wouldn't have to deal with the feelings. This is what I thought, and I was wrong.

When you take this approach to life, you cling to those who love, support, and approve of you and ignore those who do not. The problem is there is no growth. People are shunned, but the feelings and the belief, "I am not enough," remain. Eventually, I concluded I needed to be fixed.

This was my journey: pursuit of excellence, ignore those who reminded me of what I believed about myself—I am not enough, and then maintenance. This approach to life had promise, but there was only one problem. Maintenance implies something is broken, and the more I tried to fix myself, the more convinced I became that I was broken.

The years progressed and my interior life moved in circles, expanding little. There was much effort, but no matter how much maintenance I performed on myself, a belief remained—"I am not enough."

The Sacred Human

A balanced life requires the opening of two dimensions of self: our intellectual and feeling natures. My intellect was open, but my feeling nature was closed. Hiding emotions was reinforced by sports. If I was hit by a pitch while playing baseball, I did not even rub the injured spot. I just jogged to first base. The Navy also stressed the suppression of feelings. I remember talking to someone about an issue in my life. The person responded, "Sounds like a personal problem to me." In other words, personal problems have no place in the Navy, suck it up and do your job.

It was strange that while in the Navy my feeling nature was suppressed, but at the same time my caring self, my ministerial self, grew stronger. Some of the men I supervised had problems: financial, alcohol, and mental. I enjoyed visiting them, trying to help them. I was at the hospital when one of my men had his stomach pumped. I helped another with financial assistance for his family through special services, and I visited another who had a mental breakdown.

At my Navy going-away party in Philippines, I told my fellow officers I loved being with them and flying, but what I enjoyed most was the men and trying to help them. This was why I was leaving the Navy and becoming a minister.

Unity School of Religious Studies

In 1974 I entered ministerial school at Unity Village near Lee's Summit, Missouri. To my surprise and consternation, my feeling nature began to open. During prayer and meditation, I sometimes teared up or cried out of one eye. A counselor told me that this indicated cleansing was taking place at depth in me. Perhaps this was true because my life was changing, and changing rapidly.

I cried during talks I gave in speech class. I tried to suppress my feelings and stifle my tears during a moving Silent Unity prayer service and burst a blood vessel in the back of my left eye. To this day, I have a slight gray spot in the center of the vision of this eye. I think it is my thorn in the flesh reminding me to be fully human, fully alive.

The opening of my feeling nature was like the swinging of a pendulum. At first, there were few feelings. The pendulum was locked to one side, the intellectual side. When it swung to the feeling side, emotions erupted like a geyser. Feelings overwhelmed me. It took years, but eventually the pendulum swung back and forth and achieved a precarious balance that enabled me to feel what needed to be felt, but to continue to think constructively and respond calmly and responsively to life's joys and challenges. However, the pendulum still swung back and forth, and I still circled in place because I had not yet met Dawnna.

From Perfectionism to Maintenance to Acceptance

In 1988 I became the senior minister of Unity Temple on the Plaza, the founder's church of the Unity Movement. It was a magnificent building with magnificent people, some of whom remembered the founders, Charles and Myrtle Fillmore. Nancy and I and our two sons, Jamie and Ben lived in the manse that was attached to the church building. I stepped from the hallway of our home into my office.

One day, I looked closely at the faded black mailbox outside our front door. I thought it was in need of a coat of paint, but I discovered it was not painted; it was tarnished. Beneath the oxidation was copper and brass. I removed it from the wall and had professionals restore it to its former glory. One Sunday, I stood before the congregation with the restored mailbox and said it reminded me of them, that it had been tarnished, but beneath the tarnish was incredible beauty. I told the congregation that the mailbox would be mounted on the outside of my office door. It was for love notes and class papers. There were to be no complaints placed in the mailbox. All complaints were to come to me through face-to-face conversations and meetings.

I was at Unity Temple on the Plaza for a short time before moving to Unity Village to work as an executive vice president; however, not long before we moved to Unity's World Headquarters, I met a woman who changed my life. (She gave me permission to tell her story.) Dawnna met with me for counseling. She explained she was seventy pounds overweight and needed help shedding the excess pounds. In the past, I would have given her affirmations and denials to work with and probably talked with her about using her imagination to see herself the way she wanted to be, but this time I said, *"It really doesn't matter whether you lose or gain weight. What is most important is that you know you are a child of God, a spiritual being."* We talked for a time, prayed together and she left. It wasn't long afterwards that I moved to Unity Village to work, and I lost contact with Dawnna.

A year later, Dawnna wrote a note telling me she had lost the seventy pounds. I wrote back—wonderful, let's get together at the Unity Inn and share a meal together. During our meal, Dawnna explained what happened to her. She said that during our counseling session when I said it didn't really matter if she lost the weight or not, what she took away from the meeting was that I accepted her as she was. It was the beginning of Dawnna's self-acceptance. The more she accepted herself as she was, the more weight she lost. I finally saw it. The key was not maintenance; it was acceptance. A seed was planted that is still growing today.

Often, I process ideas through writing. In July, 1994, I wrote an article about self-acceptance as a key to personal transformation. Later, I was commissioned by the Unity Movement Advisory Council to write a book that became *A Daily Guide to Spiritual Living.* The book takes the reader on a year-long journey of spiritual growth from divine discontent to Paul's state of mind, "…I have learned in whatever state I am, to be content" (Philippians 4:11). Each week there is a different theme or focus. One of those weeks was entitled "The Sacred Human."

As I explored the sacred human, memories emerged. When Jamie, our older son, was two years old, he was walking down the hallway of our home. Nancy was walking behind him. She heard him say, "I love you."

Nancy replied, "Thank you. I love you, too."

Jamie answered, "I wasn't talking to you. I was talking to me." Now that's self-acceptance. Jamie realized he was a sacred human long before I did.

As I accepted myself, I looked at my humanity differently. Prior to discovering that my humanity is sacred and precious, I thought it needed to be fixed, repaired, redeemed and in some instances eliminated. A revelation came to me that is one of the most important breakthroughs of my life. In prayer and meditation, these thoughts moved through my mind, *"Unless you are willing to accept your humanity, you won't be able to express your divinity."*

For many years, I poured energy into changing and transforming my humanity. It never worked. For instance, there was a rage in me. I tried to contain it, suppress it, and purge it from my being, but I could not. When it emerged, it was like a storm. One day, Nancy and I were at my mother's home in New Orleans. Nancy and my sister, Marcella, were in the living room. I was nearby trying to put a charcoal grill together. It was not going well. The emotional storm erupted, and I threw the grill across the room. Nancy and Marcella quietly left the room. I did not rage like my father, but the storm roared through my world and in the world of those around me. It did not subside until I learned to accept the darkness of my soul.

This revelation of the power of acceptance shifted my focus and efforts. I saw that love was the answer, but love's first action is acceptance. My past noble efforts were misplaced. I tried to perform maintenance on myself when what was needed was acceptance.

Eagerly, I embarked upon this new path honoring my humanity, allowing myself to feel, no longer suppressing emotions or ignoring those people who reminded me I was not enough, and what I found was that a divine potential naturally rose up from within me. When we suppress our emotions, we can become depressed. When we try to push our feelings aside, they often ambush us, rising up and expressing themselves when we least expect it. Grills are thrown across the room, and people are verbally assaulted. I found there was another way.

Another Way

Often, I sat quietly and rather than push aside hurtful emotions, I took the courageous step of evoking memories that brought to mind the situation that caused feelings to emerge. Rather than suppress them, I called for them to join me. It seems that when feelings no longer ambush us, their power to debilitate us is diminished. I invited the feelings and thoughts to "sit with me" and "tell me more." In other words, I accepted the memories, situations, thoughts, and feelings. I did not try to change them or heal them, only to look at them and acknowledge they were part of my inner life. The truth is this: acceptance is enough, love is enough. Isn't it interesting that my spiritual journey took me from the lie that I am not enough to the truth that love is enough?

We are born of water and Spirit, and our humanity plays an important role in the expression of our true identity. As we bring love to bear and accept ourselves as we are, the divinity emerges without effort on our part because it is natural for the "divine light" to shine. As the idea of self-acceptance became clearer and clearer, I prepared to write a book about this important spiritual insight.

During my time of inner turmoil in Spokane, Washington, Nancy and I formed a not-for-profit corporation named Inner Journey. The void and lack of balance I felt turned me to God as I yearned to express more fully. There was so much in me longing to be expressed. I was sad because I was not expressing my full potential. I wanted to live a mystical life and write and teach about my discoveries.

Inner Journey was created to share mystical teachings through letters, newsletters, pamphlets, books and retreats. We had a large mailing list, and as I began writing *The Sacred Human*, I asked our Inner Journey friends, friends of God as we called ourselves, to share their experiences with self-acceptance. The result was *The Sacred Human.*

Will You Accept Me As I Am?

During Inner Journey's first retreat, people attended from around the world. The evening of the first day of the gathering, we had a candlelight service. We sat in a circle with a candle on a pedestal as our center. I spoke about the power and sacredness of our humanity and the need to accept ourselves, and then I asked the retreatants to accept me. I said, "Will you accept me just the way I am?" In unison they responded, "We accept you just the way you are." Then each person in turn stood in the center of the circle and asked the same question. Each person heard the reply, "We accept you just the way you are." There were tears, and we laid a loving foundation for our three-day gathering. Often later in the retreat when someone shared a life experience, someone in the group would say, "We accept you just the way you are." Heads nodded and at times we laughed, but in the midst of the smiles, nodding heads and words, there was acceptance. We gathered as sacred humans.

You Are Precious To God

There were two brothers, Cain and Abel. Cain thought God loved his brother more than God loved him, so Cain slew Abel. Cain was banished to the Land of Nod. According to the *Metaphysical Bible Dictionary* by Charles Fillmore, Nod means wandering, so Cain was living a purposeless, aimless life. Cain feared for his life and the fulfillment of the law, "An eye for an eye." Cain killed his brother and feared someone would kill him.

God placed a mark on Cain that was a message to all who saw him—do not harm this one. I speculate that Cain wandered aimlessly. He begged for food and drink. One day, Cain knocked on the door of a house, and when the landlord opened the door, he was repulsed by what he saw. Cain was filthy and wide-eyed, but then the person saw the mark of Cain. He invited the wanderer into his home. The host fed Cain and clothed him and sent him on his way. Cain was puzzled. Why was he treated with respect?

The host saw God's mark on Cain, "Don't harm this one; he is precious to Me." This was Cain's problem, and his problem is often ours. Cain did not know he was precious to God (We know he was precious to God because of the mark, because even though he killed his brother, Cain's life was preserved.). We, too, are precious and valued, but we often deny this truth because of what we have done or said or because of what was done or said to us. Acceptance sets us free. It may begin with others accepting us, but it must eventually become self-acceptance.

At another Inner Journey retreat, we shared another sacred human experience—an avenue of fire-lit votive candles. Each person "walked through the fire," the challenges of daily life, and stood before a basket on a pedestal filled with dark stones. Each retreatant took a dark stone representing the parts of ourselves needing to be accepted and walked on.

After the ceremony, I told the retreatants that I often carry a dark stone in my pocket. Each time I reach inside and touch it, I remember the darkness of my soul, how precious I am to God, the sacredness of my humanity and the role and power of acceptance in my life. The dark stone is like ore that is precious even though it is not apparent; it does not shine like gold. To touch the stone is to realize the mark of Cain is upon us all, for our Creator is saying to the world, "Don't harm this one; this one is precious to Me."

The sacred human is one of the most important revelations of my life. It reminds me that I am born of water and am destined to be born of Spirit, that I am a spiritual being having a human experience. Love conceives a human being, and loving acceptance of our humanity births our divinity.

When I am still, I hear the sacred human's chant, "Fully human, fully divine, fully alive." A memory rises once more to guide me through another day, "Unless you accept your humanity, you won't be able to express your divinity." The pendulum swings, and I find balance between being born of water and born of Spirit.

More provisions for the journey....

1. We are born of water and Spirit.
2. Unless we are willing to accept our humanity, we won't be able to express our divinity.
3. Our humanity is sacred and precious.
4. Let us invite the sacred human to sit with us, so we can feel what it feels and learn what it believes.
5. No longer do our emotions ambush us, for they are called into a consciousness of acceptance.
6. The mark of Cain is upon us all.

Come with me, for we know our humanity is sacred, and we are worthy to enter the Holy of Holies.

CHAPTER FOURTEEN

The Three Revelations

The First Revelation

Imagine the white water, waves and whirlpools, turbulent and troubled waters created where three mighty rivers converge at the same place and at the same time. I experienced this joining, this convergence in me, and found not troubled water, but still water, living water, a placid and peaceful pool calling for a pebble in a pond. Three revelations more powerful than the Mississippi, the Amazon, and the Nile converged in me and created the life I now live.

Even great rivers begin as a trickle; as they flow, they gather to themselves streams and brooks. They meander through meadows, and they tumble from rocky heights and plunge over pinnacles. The first of the three great revelations of my life came during turbulent times when I teetered and fell like a droplet of water in a waterfall.

I told you of this time earlier in this book. I tried to live in two worlds: the land of daily living, and the kingdom of heaven. I sought balance and believed I was to live with a foot in each world, but a foot in each world stretched me to the breaking point. Finally, I saw Jesus' promise of a way of life where I sought the kingdom and all else was added to me. As I solved the riddle of the kingdom of heaven, I discovered there were not two worlds; there was only one.

My quest was simplified. I yearned to become increasingly aware of the First Light and to allow my earthly experiences to flow from revelations and actions derived from my allegiance to Jesus' promise.

The Second Revelation

The second revelation was the Sacred Human. I finally saw the role my humanity played in the spiritual journey. My mistakes, misgivings, negativity, and insecurity called for acceptance. For years, I believed these human foibles needed to be either hidden or purged from my being. Later, I discovered I needed to accept them and myself as I am, warts and all.

The result of accepting and loving myself was stunning. Without any effort from me, my divinity emerged. It was as if a shell broke, and I was born again. The revelation of long ago was true: As I accept my humanity, I express my divinity.

How strange it is that we must be willing to touch the darkness of our humanity before we can assume our role as lights of the world. In this instance, darkness is not the absence of light; it is light's companion. There are not two paths, one dark and the other the sunlit way. Shadows and light are eternally joined. Where there are shadows, there is light. We are born of water and Spirit. We are human. We are divine.

Through acceptance and love, the sacred human and the light of the world merge to reveal the truth of being. Love expressing as acceptance leads the way, and we experience the power of kindness and compassion. It dwells in two hearts, the heart of the one who is kind and compassionate and the heart of the one who receives the gifts of kindness and compassion.

Typically, we associate spiritual experiences with the true self. We see ourselves as we truly are, like my dream after donating a kidney to Carl Osier. The vortex of light led me to a vision of the unity of all things, and the truth that all things are alive with the First Light. However, I now know that it is just as much a spiritual experience to see the truth about our humanity. Such a vision can seem to crush us, to reveal how insecure and mean we have been, but this revelation calls for self-acceptance and love. Once we get beyond the regret, shame, and guilt, love leads the way.

We then know the meaning of Jesus' insight that we are born of water and Spirit. Our humanity is the womb, and when it is bathed in love, the light of the world is born.

This realization is one of the greatest spiritual breakthroughs of my life. Two mighty rivers join, and there is purpose, and there is love. There are not two paths to walk, there is only one. There are not two of me, one human and one divine, there is only one. It takes a man and a woman to conceive a child, and it takes two births, one human and one divine, to conceive the child envisioned by the First Light. Only a child born of water and Spirit, only a child whose humanity is known to be sacred can live and shine as the light of the world.

Two rivers are joined, but there is another. The convergence is not yet complete.

The Third Revelation

The third revelation is personal. It occurs when every child achieves self-realization and declares "I am;" however, the root of this knowing stems not from the birth of a child, but from creation, from the beginning, from the First Light that declared *I am that I am.*

In the Judeo-Christian world, the first record of a human being discovering the true nature of the Creator is Moses, standing before the burning bush. His feet were bare, his mind stripped of its so-called knowledge. What he experienced was not just a bush perpetually burning; he experienced the light of creation—pure consciousness.

I do not know how long it took Moses to grasp the message of God as consciousness, but the human family does not yet know this truth. It is not because we fail to stand on the slopes of Mount Horeb; it is because we are not alone with ourselves. Until we are still, until we seek the kingdom, until we accept our humanity, we will not discover that the image and likeness in which we are made is consciousness. This is one of life's greatest revelations. It is the convergence of the third river, and it immerses us in the sea of silence that my beloved wife Nancy describes as not the absence of sound, but the presence of God.

God is no longer static, all-knowing, and complete. The First Light is an ever-expanding consciousness, an explorer probing Itself and calling for us to mount the same expedition into the unknown. I call it the EEC, the Ever-Expanding Consciousness.

Three Streams of Consciousness

Three rivers, three revelations, converged to create a way of life in which silence is the teacher and revelation is what is taught. I want to retrace this part of my journey. Come with me as we listen to a preacher pray his prayer informing God about what must be done. This will be our meager beginning, but eventually we will discover prayer is not about the earth; it is about awakening, it is about conscious oneness with the cosmic consciousness of creation.

More provisions for the journey….

1. Jesus' promise: seek first the kingdom and all these things shall be added unto you.
2. The Sacred Human: Unless I am willing to accept my humanity, I will not be able to express my divinity.
3. God is ever, expanding consciousness.

Come, let us listen to the pastoral prayer of the preacher.

CHAPTER FIFTEEN

A Prayerful Journey: The Beginning

The Preacher and The Child

What I remember most about church when I was a child was the preacher's prayer.

It began: *Hear our prayer, O Lord* and continued as the preacher informed God of the many problems facing the world and members of the congregation. *There's war and pestilence in the land, O God. We need your help. Come down from on high and work your miracles. We are helpless, Mighty God. You are powerful; you are power, the power to do all things. There is unrest in the cities and fear in people's hearts. Erase our greed and self-centeredness and purge our minds and hearts of that which is not like you.* The prayer went on and on, informing God of the actions needed.

It always concerned me when the preacher stopped speaking. I'd open an eye and look at him. The silence opened my heart to the minister because I thought he had forgotten what to say. From this pastoral prayer experience, I concluded prayer was words, prayer was something we do, and prayer's purpose was getting God's help with earthly issues.

As a Boy Scout, I prayed such a prayer. Our troop was to perform during the half-time show at the North-South Senior Bowl football game in Mobile, Alabama. In preparation for this important event and without permission, we cut down bamboo poles from the back of a man's property; a strange thing for trustworthy and honest Boy Scouts to do in preparation for a public event—steal. I could hear the buckshot hitting the bamboo when the owner fired into the tree tops. Needless to say, we were in trouble, so it was time for prayer, a bargaining prayer, in which I promised to become a minister, if God would get me and my fellow scouts out of trouble. I have wondered if this "prayer" had anything to do with my chosen career path as a minister.

The trouble passed and we cut the bamboo, so we could lash the poles together and build a thirty-foot tower during the half-time show. I dressed as a Native American because I performed a buffalo dance with some of my fellow scouts as the tower was built. Then I climbed to the top of the completed structure with signal flags and spelled out "welcome" to the crowd. Childhood is a hoot. There wasn't much prayer, but when I did pray it was earnest, because there was a problem that needed divine attention and intervention.

Nancy and I once talked to Ben, our younger son, about church attendance when he was five years old. He did not want to go to church. We tried to apply adult logic to convince him to attend. After all, I was the minister. We said, "What if God wants to tell you something?"

Ben answered, "I talk to God on Friday."

We responded, "What if God wants to talk to you on another day?"

Ben's answer brought a smile to our lips. "Tell Him I didn't do it?"

When we moved to Kansas City and I became the minister of Unity Temple on the Plaza, we worked hard to unpack our belongings and bring order to our new home. One evening, we were exhausted, and we asked Ben if he would meditate with us for a few minutes.

Ben reluctantly sat with Nancy and me. After our time in silence, I asked our young eight-year-old son if he heard any message from God during our quiet time. He answered, "No, God was mumbling."

I thought, "Well, that's a start," but then Nancy and I realized that Nancy, who was exhausted, fell asleep during our quiet time and was mumbling. Obviously, we progress through some interesting stages on our journey to understand God as an ever-expanding consciousness.

Different Prayer, Same Purpose

The Rosemergys were church goers. My dad often served as a lay Methodist minister along with his job as a marine inspector, and my mother wouldn't think of missing church on Sunday. I followed the family tradition even when I was in college; however, most of my time in church was as a sponsor with the MYF, Methodist Youth Fellowship, supporting teenagers in their spiritual journey. While in college, I brought my girlfriends to the MYF group I served. Nancy was one of those girlfriends. The young teenagers loved having college students as their sponsors. I remember taking our group on an overnight rally with other youth groups. I had to sleep on the floor in front of the boys' sleeping room to keep them away from the girls.

Remember in chapter nine I told you about my introduction of Unity? I attended church with my parents in the oddly shaped building on Saint Charles Street in New Orleans. After a moving service by Rev. Ruth Murphy, the first female minister I had ever seen, I went to the church bookstore and purchased Unity's primary textbook, *Lessons in Truth* by H. Emilie Cady. It was the first Unity book ever published. Dr. Cady opened my eyes to another way of life and in particular to another way of prayer—affirmative prayer. It was based on Jesus' statement in Mark 11:24. "Therefore I tell you, whatever you ask in prayer, believe that you will receive it and it will be yours."

Affirmative prayer appealed to me. There was no begging. The words were a prayer of faith and thanksgiving because the desired outcome was declared accomplished. "It is done, and so it is" often sealed the prayer, but the prayer was still words. It was something we did. We prayed affirming what we wanted and what we wanted was usually of the world. The crops needed rain, someone needed healing. A job or sum of money was urgently required. The form of the prayer had changed, but the motivation and desired result was like that of the preacher.

Justification for this approach to prayer was abundant. "Ask, and it will be given to you; seek, and you will find; knock, and it will be opened to you" (Matthew 7:7). If I wanted something, I asked for it. And yet the sign of something more was present. "...for it is the Father's good pleasure to give you the kingdom" (Luke 12:32). Isn't it interesting how consciousness is a glass through which we see, and we see what we want to see; we see only what our consciousness allows us to see.

In these early days, I interpreted Jesus' statement about God's pleasure to mean that God wanted for me what I wanted for myself. God wanted me to prosper, to be healed and to have loving relationships. These human desires were my focus and the focus of my affirmative prayers. And they seemed to work—most of the time, but it was disconcerting to get what I wanted, and it was not enough. I thought I had it all, but I knew something was missing.

This was anguish. I was not content. Undoubtedly, it was part of my ongoing struggle of not being enough, but there was something deeper moving within me. Nancy often said to me that she did not understand my discontent. "You have what most people want, and you are not happy." Her statement captured exactly what concerned me the most. It was the feeling at the center of the struggle to live between two worlds. It called for not another prayer practice, but a change in intention and purpose, taking me beyond "added things" to the kingdom of God that is God's pleasure to give to all of humanity.

My Evolving Prayer Practice

My first prayer practices mirrored the prayer of the preacher, informing God about compelling needs and what appeared to be overlooked. The world needed peace, my friend needed healing, and his father needed a job. These unresolved issues, these unanswered prayers caused me to question God's nature. Why doesn't God respond? Surely, peace and healing and security are God's will for everyone. Is God angry with me, angry with humanity? Is the Creator punishing us or simply detached from human needs? Why the reluctance? Is God lazy or slothful?

My own problems caused me to alter my prayer practice from begging to bargaining. My prayer was a conversation outlining the "deal." "If you get me out of this dilemma, I'll do this…."

Years later, affirmative prayer held promise. It did not attempt to change God, it promised to change me, to change my consciousness, so what I wanted could come into being. The object of the prayer was no longer to get God to act; it was a way of transforming my consciousness, and my transformed consciousness would then manifest itself in a way that resolved my challenge. Prayer at this stage of my journey was not a way of life; it was a way of fixing and repairing my life. I was still bound to the preacher's prayer; something in the world needed maintenance.

More provisions for the journey….

1. A prayer life is a progression, a journey in consciousness from one insight to another, from one experience to another.
2. Most of us believe prayer is something we do; that prayer is words, and its focus and purpose is our earthly lives.

3. The form and practice of prayer may change, but it often has the same focus, the resolution of our human problems and challenges.
4. Affirmative prayer is a prayer of thanksgiving because it affirms that what we desire is already ours; its declaration is: it is done.

This was the beginning of my prayer and meditative life. This beginning does not resemble where I am in consciousness now, but every journey to a high place begins in a valley. Come with me, let us go higher, let us discover God's pleasure.

CHAPTER SIXTEEN

A Prayerful Journey Continues
The Second Day

The Question

What needs changing, the world, God or me? In the beginning, on the first day of the creation of my prayer life, I thought the world needed changing, and prayer's purpose was to get God to change it. On the second day of the creation of my contemplative life, I realized I needed changing, not God. God was not lazy or slothful. God was not detached from me or the world. God was not angry with humanity or vengeful.

The issue was not God; it was me. I needed to be transformed; my mind needed to be renewed. "Do not be conformed to the world, but be transformed by the renewing of your mind…." (Romans 12:2). Affirmative prayer, it seemed, was the answer. It would be the hands that molded me, so round and round on the potter's wheel I went. The wheel was an ancient law first known as "like begets like" and updated in the latter part of the 19th century to The Law of Mind Action: "Thoughts held in mind produce after their kind." Seeds no longer lay in furrows in fields; they sprouted in my mind and bore fruit of every kind. The harvest was not solely a series of happenings, conditions, and experiences. The harvest was more; it was my life, and I was its master if I could master my subconscious mind.

This hidden mind governed the autonomic functions of my body, causing my heart to beat and hormones to secrete without conscious thought from me. Like a hidden cave or vault, it housed my memories, beliefs, regrets, and my deepest shame and guilt. The belief, I am not enough, occupied a space here for many years. My attitudes about life and people rose from this shadowy place. Truths lived here beside lies, as well as memories and conclusions I surmised from the things that happened to me and the things I did.

The truths and those things lovely, pure, and just within the subconscious mind were affirmed, and the lies were purged and declared powerless. The best of me was lifted up, and the worst of me no longer influenced my life. This is what I thought. And I was wrong.

The Affirmative Way

At the time, the affirmative way made sense. I could retain what is true and banish forever from my consciousness what is not true. Later, I discovered that I had not purged all error from my consciousness, I had driven it deeper into the cave, farther into the darkness where I thought certain events and beliefs belonged. Surely, they would not find their way through the labyrinth of my consciousness to my conscious mind and my life, but they did.

I had not yet met Dawnna and was not yet acquainted with the sacred human I told you about earlier. Little did I know that even my humanity, its darkness and its lies, have value, that they would cause the dawning of another day of creation of my prayer life. But that's for another time later in the week of creation, another chapter in *An Autobiography of a Christian Heretic.*

The second day of the creation of my contemplative life was a long one. The subconscious mind needed to be conditioned, so my mind could be renewed and my life transformed.

The subconscious mind needed to be informed of the error of its ways and to be told the truth and told the truth often. My prayer practice was filled with words, with affirmations that declared the truth as I understood it, and denials that said no to lies and purged my hidden mind of errors and untruths. This kind of prayer practice is repetitious because the subconscious mind learns the truth through hearing, speaking, singing, intoning, and living it again and again. And so, I spoke the truth as I understood it, and denied the power of people, conditions, and false beliefs over me. I memorized popular affirmations such as: *I am a spiritual being living in a spiritual universe governed by spiritual laws,* and denials such as: *Nothing disturbs the calm peace of my soul.* Literally, I held hundreds if not thousands of statements of truth in my mind.

I took control. I was the master of my ship. The potter's wheel was spinning, but just because I was moving didn't mean I was getting anywhere. Where there are circles, there is movement, there is repetition, but I was not far from where the potter first placed his hands upon me.

Transformation was under way. There was progress, but the emphasis was on my outer world, on what was happening around me. My spiritual practice was primarily to enhance my outer conditions and my earthly life. The path seemed clear, but then I met the mystics, and they introduced me to another path I did not even know existed. I began to understand Jesus' statement that He did not come to bring peace, but a sword. This sword did not bring death; it brought life. It did not strike at other people. It struck at me, for it challenged preconceived ideas and beliefs. It created inner conflict, evidence of the dismantling of one way of life and the prospect of another way to live. This inner conflict did bring war, and it was a harbinger of peace. An inner conflict lived on the second day of the creation of my contemplative life, but it eventually led me to the third day.

The Mystics

I don't know why I did it, but I picked up Evelyn Underhill's book, *Mysticism,* that outlined the five steps of the mystical way of life. I was fascinated by step four, the dark night of the soul. I heard people speak of it during their darkest times, but I discerned that the dark night of the soul was not a difficult time in a person's earthly life; it was a dark time when we lost our conscious connection with God. The only way beyond the darkness was love, to commit to love the Creator even though we are convinced we will never know our God again.

Equally, I longed for the Unitive Life, a life of conscious oneness with the ever-expanding consciousness God is. Of course, at that time, I knew nothing of God as consciousness. There was only God, a word that encompassed so many things I longed for and yet did not understand. Reading *Mysticism* revealed a path; I wanted to walk it, but it was only words on a page and a hunger in my heart. I felt a divine touch; I felt a nudge, and it led me beyond the five steps of the mystical path to the lives of the mystics.

I read about them: European priests, nuns, monks, and lay people, poets, philosophers, desert fathers, Sufis, and the masters of the far east. Their religions differed, the cultures and images used to explain their experiences varied, but there was the common ground of solitude, silence and revelation. Jesus prayed and fasted for forty days in the wilderness, and the desert fathers lived their lives in this barren land. Buddha found enlightenment under the Bodhi tree, and Mohammed gained direction in a cave on what Muslims call the night of power. The common quest for the Ever-Expanding Consciousness was evident in their lives and their spiritual practices.

I knew their path; I was acquainted with their lives, and now it was time to read not about them, but what they had written about their struggles and discoveries. I plunged into *The Cloud of Unknowing,* an anonymous work, *The Life,* by St. Teresa of Avila, *The Ascent of Mount Carmel* and *The Dark Night of the Soul* by

Saint John of the Cross, the poetry of Rumi, etc. *The Prophet* by Kahil Gibran was especially moving. I had a recording, a dramatic reading of *The Prophet* by actor Richard Harris. I laid on the floor of our living room at night and listened and wept. And there was more, much more, and the more I read the more I found myself in a metaphysical desert.

I trekked and rested in stillness and discovered that the expansive emptiness of a desert can hold a person's pain and longing, that deserts are not empty; they are filled with what we bring with us. Silence is not the absence of sound, and solitude is not being alone; it is discovering ourselves and the treasure of our souls that resides in the dark cave of our humanity. Within the darkness are precious stones. They don't glisten like gold, because they are ore needing to be refined in the furnace and blinding light of the desert and in the warmth and acceptance of divine love. It is here that our humanity is known to be sacred and precious.

Imagine a mind filled with such thoughts and at the same time filled with the needs and demands of daily living—divine longing and loneliness living together in the same world with loving family and friends. This is what I described to you earlier as living in two worlds.

Then It Happened

While serving as the minister of Unity Church of Truth in Spokane, Washington, I conducted a prayer retreat for the members of the church's prayer ministry. During an afternoon break, I went to my room and rested on my cot. I was not praying/meditating. I was resting, and a strange thought came to me. *Jim, you don't have to condition your subconscious mind anymore.* Oh, I thought. *Yes, because you have the mind of the Christ.*

I sat up. That's it. I would be a fool to try to condition the Christ Mind that lived in me. It did not need to be conditioned; it needed to be unleashed. In that moment, I stopped trying to condition my subconscious mind. The vain repetition that Jesus cautioned about ended, but how was I to understand the Law of Mind Action, thoughts held in mind produce after their kind? And what of the spiritual tools of affirmation and denial? Was I to toss them aside?

I was about to enter into the third day of the creation of my prayer life, but not quite yet. My purpose was changing—no more conditioning of the subconscious mind to meet the challenges of daily living. Now I was to unleash the Christ Mind, but how? What tools would I use? Were tools necessary? Could there be a union of my current spiritual practices and what I was learning of the mystical path? Yes.

The Law of Mind Action

Two things happened. First, my purpose in prayer/meditation changed. It was no longer about my earthly life. The intent became conscious oneness with God. The oneness poem of long ago was now front and center in my contemplative life. I saw that Jesus' interior life centered on His prayer, "I and the Father are one." Long ago, I saw this prayer; it touched me and I sensed its importance, but it was not until I encountered the mystics that I knew this was to be a driving force in my life.

Secondly, my prayer practice changed. A word in the Law of Mind Action took on new meaning: held. Thoughts HELD in mind produce after their kind. Previously, through repetition, I held affirmations and denials in my mind like prisoners in a dungeon. It was as if I were afraid to turn them loose or to lose them. Their purpose was to condition the subconscious mind, to hammer it with truth.

Now I no longer gripped the truth I declared, I let it rest in my hand; I let it rest in my mind. My practice was not a fist; it was an open hand, a palm turned upward. I still used my old friends, affirmations and denials, but not as a hammer to pound the truth deep inside me or to crumble error into its innate nothingness. Now affirmations and denials lifted me up; they were like a wind on a mountain cliff rising higher and higher, lifting me like a bird with outstretched wings. I called this prayer practice "putting on my wings."

At first, I thought this new prayer practice could lift me into conscious oneness with God, but it didn't. Such an effort was a repeat of the building of the Tower of Babel. No human being by his own effort can lift himself into an awareness of the ever-expanding consciousness God is. Affirmations and denials lifted me, but they could lift me no higher than the apex of human consciousness.

This apex is like a high meadow on a mountain, a beautiful place. We can see what we have never seen before, but it is not the summit of the mountain. There is only one who can take us higher—Grace. We will meet her in the next chapter.

Resting In The High Meadow

I had been in the desert; now I was called to the mountains. While serving at Unity Church of Truth in Spokane, Washington I asked if I could have three days each quarter for a personal time of prayer/meditation, contemplation and reflection. The board of the ministry lovingly supported me in this request.

I met a nun, Sister Florence Leone, who facilitated a retreat center called Kairos House. Kairos is a Greek word meaning momently or in the moment. On the grounds of the retreat center, on a ridge, were small "A" frame hermitages. I climbed the ridge to my hermitage, and it was the starting place for another ascent to the High Meadow. I took my own food and only a pen and stenographer's notebook to record my thoughts and insights. I took no books; I did not even read the Bible. I rested and walked and sat and watched the deer and allowed my five senses to bring me to Kairos, to the moment.

This was where I learned to wait, and it transformed me. I will tell you more about waiting in the next chapter, but these times of coming apart awhile lifted me in consciousness until I felt an urge to write *The Watcher.*

I remember the spring day when I sat in a lounge chair on the back deck of our home in Spokane. Mount Spokane was in the distance, snow still on the summit. I had my steno pad and a pencil and words started to flow. It had been a long time since I wrote a manuscript with a pen or pencil. The computer was my friend now, but *The Watcher* was different. It was prose poetry. Words flowed like water. This is how *The Watcher* began…

> *With aloneness as her companion and silence as her teacher, the Watcher had waited. For twelve thousand years, a blind sister had stretched her soul to sense the light. Now, for the appointed twelve days, light streaked across her mind, etching the long-awaited message.*
>
> *In an ancient time, before remembering, the first Watcher waited. As death extended new life to her, she put aside quietude and spoke of His coming to a sister made blind so she might see. In this way, the promise of a new world passed from sister to sister, each a symbol of the deepest yearning in us.*
>
> *Now the joy anticipated by each Watcher filled the soul of this blind sister.*
>
> *With her being suspended in timelessness and her mind as a still pool awaiting the wind, she sensed His coming.*
>
> *She knew of waiting, but now the light proclaimed His coming. What was she to do? The dying sister who spoke to her spoke not of doing. The instruction was to weave her mind into the fabric of the universe and to wrap herself in a cocoon of Silence.*

She closed her sightless eyes and heard the voice that rushed upon her like a storm twelve days ago.

"Go to the city of peace where all people are children."

In the way made known to Watchers, her body became a radiant light encircling the earth. Then all the points of light converged on Jerusalem.

That's the way it began. I wrote as quickly as I could with the words pouring from the pencil clutched in my hand. Most of the book was written this way. The experience was tactile as well as mental, emotional and spiritual. I felt every word as I moved the pencil to inscribe the letters.

I yearned for a contemplative life. The three days I was away each quarter prepared me for the challenges and joys of the expansion of my interior life. Spokane and the dear friends I met there and the beauty of the area did their work. Change was coming. I could feel it.

Unity Temple On The Plaza

In 1988, Nancy and I and the boys left Spokane when I assumed the leadership of the founder's church in Kansas City, Missouri. This ministry was the stream of consciousness first developed by the co-founders of the Unity Movement, Charles and Myrtle Fillmore. I was only there a short time, fifteen months, but it was a time of deepening with a continuation of the times of silence and contemplation.

I found a retreat center facilitated by a gifted musician who was a priest who allowed me to cloister at one of their hermitages. Once again, I brought my own food, no books, only my steno pad and pencil. I spoke to no one. I scheduled times at this spiritual center months in advance.

Prior to one of my visits to the hermitage, Connie Fillmore, president of Unity School of Christianity and a ministerial school classmate, called me and invited me to dinner. It was to be a conversation between just the two of us, and she said she wanted to talk to me about my destiny. That got my attention.

We met and talked. During our dinner, she invited me to come to work at Unity Village as an Executive Vice President with responsibilities in Education, Publishing, International, Human Resources, and Maintenance. I told Connie I needed forty days of prayer and meditation to contemplate her offer. Amazingly, the forty-day period ended at the conclusion of a previously scheduled three-day personal retreat at the hermitage.

I rested in silence at the retreat center for three days, and the decision came with ease. I did not ask if I should leave Unity Temple on The Plaza to work at Unity Village. I simply gave attention to the kingdom of God, to awakening to an awareness of the Presence. I knew that if I experienced God as wisdom and light, guidance would be "added" to me. I eventually came to call this prayerful process not decision making, but decision letting.

I let the light shine, and I left Unity Temple on The Plaza and joined my colleagues at Unity Village.

My nearly twelve-year tenure of service to the Unity Movement at Unity World Headquarters was a time of trial and great growth. It required that I expand my consciousness from thoughts of self, a ministry or the collection of Unity ministries called the Association of Unity Churches, to the Unity Worldwide Movement. I learned new administrative skills, and brought my leadership skills to bear as never before.

During this time, Nancy and I built a lake home we called the High Meadow at Sunrise Beach, Missouri, at Lake of the Ozarks. Our home was on a bluff 80 feet above the water. My study was on the second floor of the cabin overlooking two branches of the lake, truly a place of beauty and creativity.

Here I saw and experienced the dawn of the third day of my contemplative life. Here I learned to watch and wait.

More provisions for the journey….

1. On the first day of the creation of my prayer life, I sought to change God, to get God to act and do my bidding.
2. On the second day of the creation of my prayer life, I knew it was me who needed to change.
3. At first, I thought the purpose of affirmative prayer was to condition my subconscious mind and bring about what I needed and wanted.
4. Later, the purpose of affirmative prayer was to lift me up in consciousness to the apex of my human consciousness. It was to unleash the mind of God in me.
5. Reading about the mystical path, the lives of the mystics and their writings, changed my purpose for prayer/meditation and my prayer/meditation practice.
6. On the second day of the creation of my prayer life, I held truth in me like it was a prisoner that might escape. Later, I learned to hold the truth gently in my mind, to rest with it until I was lifted to the apex of my human consciousness. This is a beautiful, positive, lovely place, but it is not the summit of the mystical mountain.

Come, the summit of the mountain awaits.

CHAPTER SEVENTEEN

A Prayerful Journey Continues
The Third Day

Monticello Lawn

It was a beautiful day, the first day of a week of hiking and camping in the Presidential Mountain Range of New Hampshire. The highest winds ever recorded on earth lashed the summit of Mount Washington, the highest peak of the range, our ultimate goal.

We split the campers into the two groups. I led the faster group. Another counselor led the slower group. The slower group spread out and the unsupervised boys cast off the "burden" of food and tent halves. Because of the lack of food, several days into our trip, the fellow counselor and I left the boys in a lean-to and hiked to the summit of Mount Washington where there was a weather station, visitor center, and store.

We hiked in a storm because we had no choice. We needed food. We reached a place called Monticello Lawn. The clouds were dense. I leaned into the wind and walked forward twenty feet, the point where the other trip counselor and I began to lose sight of one another. The counselor walked forward to where I was, and then I walked forward another twenty feet. This practice continued until the visibility improved.

Eventually, we reached the summit of Mount Washington, bought food and began our return trek to the boys. On the way back, the weather cleared. Monticello Lawn was a high meadow with grass bent by the prevailing wind. We looked sixty miles in one direction and sixty miles in the opposite direction. It was breathtaking. I never forgot the image of Monticello Lawn. I adopted the phrase High Meadow, and it became an important part of the development of my prayer life. In fact, Nancy and I named our cabin in Lake of Ozarks the "High Meadow." Our current cabin in the mountains of Georgia is called "High Meadow II." The image of the high meadow never left me. I will tell you more about it soon, for it was central to the third day of the creation of my contemplative life.

On day one, my purpose was to change God, to get God to act on my behalf and to solve some dilemma. On day two, my purpose was not to change God; it was to change myself, to condition my subconscious mind, to affirm and deny and know the truth. Manifestation remained the ultimate goal. There was a problem to solve and a successful human life to live.

On the third day of the creation of my prayer life, I had a new purpose. I put aside problem-solving, manifestation, and "added things," and yearned for a relationship with God. I had to find a way to get to the High Meadow, a place of waiting, for waiting is the beginning of divine friendship. This is what friends do; they sit together. Sometimes they speak, sometimes they don't; always they listen.

The Gift And The Fragrance

My prayerful purpose was refined by a meditative image of the gift and the fragrance. I returned home from work, and a gift was on my doorstep. It was a gift from my best friend. I took the gift inside and opened it. It was perfect. My friend knows me so well, but suddenly sadness came upon me. Why was I sad? Because I had just missed my friend. I appreciated the gift, but what a joy it would have been to sit and talk with my friend.

The next day, I returned from work and entered my house. There was a fragrance in the air, the perfume, the cologne of my best friend. Sadness returned; I had just missed my friend and the joy of being together.

God is my best friend. The gift represents something tangible like a healing or a new job, an award, or money. It is appreciated, and it may be a gift from God, but it is not the same as the experience of the ever-expanding consciousness God is.

The fragrance is also a gift, but it is not tangible. It is an idea, a thought such as "God is enough" or a feeling such as peace or contentment. Likewise, the fragrance is appreciated; it is a gift from God, but God is what I seek. This is the change in purpose that came on the third day.

Abraham called God friend. I wanted to be God's friend, too. I wanted to pray as Jesus prayed, "I and the Father are one." On the third day, I sought the kingdom; I prayed to experience conscious oneness with the One. My prayers no longer outlined a desirable future. They declared as did Jesus' prayer, a state of being. I and the Father are one. On the third day, I called God friend.

I saw Jesus' approach to prayer in Mark 11:24. "Therefore, I tell you whatever you ask in prayer, believe you have received it, and it shall be yours." (KJV) There are many powerful words in this verse of scripture: ask, prayer, believe, receive, but the most important word is "it," because "it" determines why we pray. "It" can be a "gift," a "fragrance," a healing, a bookcase, a new job, or peace of mind. In fact, on previous days of the creation of my prayer life, I prayed for all these things, but no more. My purpose on the third day of the creation of my life of prayer was conscious awareness of God.

On the third day, I knew why I prayed/meditated. Now, I needed to know how. I needed to know how to how to climb to the High

Meadow, how to "put on my wings," and how to wait patiently at the airport for a friend. I will explain all of these images and how they guided me to the third day of the creation of my contemplative life.

The Ascent To The High Meadow

Day three of the creation of my prayer life dawned when I discovered that affirmations and denials are not just statements; they are ways of life. Through the affirmative process, states of consciousness form in us; attitudes and beliefs develop. Through the process of denial, we cast off thoughts, attitudes, and beliefs. Every thought, word, and image we hold in mind and every action affirms and denies either truth or error. Ideally, we know the truth and cleanse our consciousness of lies and error, but these approaches to life are neutral and impersonal; they can help us or hinder us. Sometimes we deny truth and affirm error.

Affirmation says yes. Denial says no or be gone. We can affirm the truth, say yes to truth, or we can say yes to lies and error. We can say no; we can deny negative beliefs a place in our consciousness, or we can deny the truth of our being. We can believe truth or lies. We can say no to truth just as surely as we say no to error. The affirmative life builds up; it embraces. Denial tears down; it releases what was built up.

Ideally what we think, say, imagine, and do are congruent; they unite and declare the truth, but there are times when what we say is not what we think, and what we do is not what we say. However, life changes rapidly when our thoughts, words, imaginings and actions are in concert with one another. These are the building blocks of consciousness we put in place, and we are always building. When revelation of the ever-expanding consciousness God is becomes an additional building block of consciousness, a life of beauty, peace, joy, love, and service is lived.

Affirmation and denial are the processes of life I used to ascend the slopes of the mountain to the High Meadow. I spoke the truth and said no to lies and error. My thoughts and words united and strengthened me. At first, this was laborious work, but eventually, the climb in consciousness was a joy, and every time I climbed to the High Meadow, I was more prepared to experience the Ever-Expanding Consciousness.

The High Meadow

The High Meadow is a place to wait, but don't think of a bench in a park, a rock ledge overlooking a majestic valley, or a sandy beach in an isolated cove of blue-green water. The High Meadow is an elevated state of *human* consciousness. It lies within. It feels good when we rest in this state of being. Our thoughts are positive and constructive. There is peace, but the High Meadow is not the summit of the mountain. It is not the realm of revelation or an experience of the Ever-Expanding Consciousness we seek. I say again, the High Meadow is a place in *human* consciousness where we wait, but for whom or for what do we wait?

We wait for a "woman" to emerge from the mist and mystery of the mountain to take us by the hand and lead us to the trailhead that ascends to the summit of the mountain that is the kingdom of God, the EEC, the ever-expanding consciousness God is. The woman's name is Grace, for there is nothing we can do that will take us higher than the High Meadow. We rise to this height of human consciousness through our efforts, through our prayer/meditative practice, but we can go no higher until Grace takes us by the hand. So we wait….

Two Questions

There are two questions to ask about the High Meadow. The first is how do we get there; how do we ascend to the apex of human consciousness? Humanity has many prayer practices that lift us to this high place. We chant, intone, recite written prayers; follow our breath, read sacred writ, spin prayer wheels, observe the shimmering flame of a candle, and feel the wind in our hair and sun on our face; we walk in the woods. There are hundreds of spiritual practices that lift us up. Some are practiced in community; others we practice alone.

On the third day of the creation of my prayer life, affirmations and denials joined. Statements of truth were held in mind and error was refused entry. I rested with my thoughts; I spoke the truth, chanted or intoned the truth as I understood it. Then I waited. Each truth expressed was a step up the mountain taking me nearer to the High Meadow.

If I had a healing need, I headed for the rarified air of the High Meadow. Affirmations and denials carried me there. *I am whole; I am as the Creator created me. Nothing of the earth changes the truth of my being. I am an expression of the ever-expanding consciousness of the First Light; I am life being lived. I am that I am, the way I will always be. I am whole. I am.* Then I waited…

If I felt alone and rejected, I breathed deeply, placed my hand over my heart and held in mind… *I am united with all life, with all of creation. Whatever I am aware of is a part of me. The universe lives in me. I accept myself the way I am, and more of my true being is revealed to me. I am loved; love dwells in me and overflows into my life and the world where I live.* Then I waited….

If I had a prosperity need, I remembered: *I live in a circle of giving and receiving. It is not a prosperous life I seek; it is a life of generosity. I am the place where the divine supply appears. My heart, mind, and hands are open to give and to receive, and what is received is an awareness of the First Light. I remember I am sustained by what I cannot see with my eyes. I am generous. I am safe and secure.* Then I waited....

Whenever I faced a challenge, I donned my "climbing gear" and headed for the High Meadow. I began with an idea. If the challenge was healing, life and wholeness were the center around which affirmation and denials, my prayer practice, formed. If I experienced lack, the beginning idea was source and substance. If I felt rejected, love and forgiveness were my first steps. All things begin with an idea, so it was appropriate for my beginning to be divine ideas.

Ideally, every word, every thought, and every image of mind was a step taken toward the High Meadow, the height of my human consciousness. It felt good in this place. I was high on the mountain, high in consciousness, and I saw what I had not seen before. There was a tendency to believe I had arrived, but I had not. The High Meadow is a beautiful place, but it is not the summit of the mountain; it is a place to wait and stretch out my hand, for Grace is coming.

Put On Your Wings

Another image lifted me up. Our cabin at Sunrise Beach, Missouri sat on an eighty-foot bluff over a lake. We could see miles down two arms of the lake many people thought looked like a dragon. Often birds of prey flew by our deck on their way to catch the updraft of a nearby two-hundred-foot cliff. As they flew below us, they flapped their wings to gain energy and height, and then suddenly they "put on their wings" and waited and trusted they would be lifted by an unseen presence, the wind. I realized I, too, must stretch out my wings, wait and trust an unseen presence to lift me higher.

Learning to Wait

The first question was how do we get to the High Meadow? Our prayer/meditative practices take us there. The second question is: how do we wait, how do we trust, what do we do when our outstretched wings grow tired, or we are so tired we cannot take another step opposing the force of "gravity" that impedes our desire to rise higher?

Many people speak, chant, intone, or spin the wheel, but they do not wait, and waiting is crucial. It is more than a practice, more than an art; it is a necessity. Just as Jesus waited three days in the tomb, we must make the phrase, "wait three days" an integral part of our daily life, for waiting calls for Grace to come; waiting becomes trust, and trust becomes faith.

The fact is, waiting is difficult, so how do we wait? There are two answers to this question. The second answer will come in the next chapter, for I cannot reveal it now because it was not revealed until the fourth day of the creation of my contemplative life.

Waiting was, the great challenge on the third day of the creation of my contemplative life. The mind wandered. Thoughts, feelings, memories and images reappeared. Some were disturbing, parts of myself I hid long ago.

I forgot I am whole. My thoughts returned to the pain of rejection, grief or loss or the resounding words of a doctor's diagnosis. Fear appeared, and there was no unity. Everything was fragmented and separate. I tumbled down the mountain and had to claw my way back up to reach the High Meadow in the hope that Grace would come quickly and take me higher.

On the third day, waiting became my practice. An inner strength and persistence grew. When I fell, I got up. My prayer/meditative practice, affirmations and denials lifted me. I held them gently in mind again. Like a bird, I stretched my wings, and an unseen spirit wind lifted me.

At times, I stood on the summit. Feelings of peace flooded my being. Asking ceased. Revelations came. The Ever-Expanding Consciousness whispered, "I am enough for you," and those five words became dear friends that I held in mind again and again as I tumbled down the mountain, leaving behind the High Meadow.

My prayer practice lifted me to the High Meadow, and I waited and when the thoughts, feelings, memories, or images of the past assaulted me, I lost my footing, lost my peace and tumbled down the mountain, but I got up and held in mind once more the highest truth I knew, and I waited again.

There were times when Grace came. I shared with you insights revealed to me as I stood on the summit of the mountain. A dear friend like: "Unless you accept your humanity, you won't be able to express your divinity." Statements such as this refocused me and took me higher. I held these words in mind, and I felt my hand reach out for Grace. Sometimes she came.

On the second day, affirmation and denial hammered the truth into my subconscious mind, they stood guard and did not allow the truth to escape or lies to become rooted in consciousness. On the third day, affirmation and denial gave me strength to take another step up the slopes of the mountain or supported my outstretched wings that were longing for a spirit wind to lift me higher. At this time in my spiritual journey, affirmation and denial as processes of life were everything, but without waiting, they were nothing; however, when joined to waiting, they did their work.

Two images came to me that helped create attitudes of mind to support me as I waited for Grace or for the uplifting spirit wind.

A friend, David Davenport, flew to Fort Myers for a visit. Nancy and I arrived early at the airport and stood at the top the concourse where our friend would emerge from his plane. There was a narrow passageway where we would first see him, so this is where we focused our attention, but there were distractions. Lots of people waited with us, looking for their guests to arrive. Delightful, adorable children were jumping up and down in anticipation of arriving grandparents. I thought, "I wonder when our grandchildren will come to see us again." And then I focused on the opening where David would emerge. I did not condemn myself for my lack of focus. I simply refocused. A police officer came by on a Segway. I thought, "Hmm...that looks like fun. I wonder what they cost." And then without berating myself, I looked again at the place where we would first see David.

Waiting for Grace is like waiting for a friend at the airport. We focus and lose focus, but there is no self-condemnation. It is the way it is when we wait at the airport. Grandchildren are adorable. That's the way it is. Segways look like fun. It is what it is.

Of course, not all distractions are adorable, and our thoughts, feelings and images are sometimes more than distractions, but there is a way to wait.

Dear Friends

Help came not from my human consciousness, but from the ever-expanding consciousness God is. The help, the revelations, became dear friends, never forgotten and held close to my heart. These dear friends were different from statements I read or were given. They were God gifts, the strongest encouragement to take another step. They were the hands that supported my outstretched wings when I tired of waiting. Moses needed help when he extended his staff to sustain the wind that parted the waters of the Red Sea, and I needed help when I tired of waiting or when waiting seemed fruitless.

Six Words

Six words helped me during the most challenging time of waiting; a time when hurtful memories returned, negative thoughts encircled me, or a challenge dominated my mind. In the midst of such times, six words appeared and became my dearest friends: *It is; God is, I am.*

On the third day when the mind darted from place to place and a challenge with all its feelings and thoughts grew tall and commanded my attention, I remembered my dearest friends. When I began to doubt myself or condemn what was emerging from within me, the six words, *It is; God I; I am* refocused my attention.

Of the healing challenge, the grief, the sense of insecurity or lack, I said, "It is." I did not label it bad or good. "It is." It exists for now, but it is not eternal. It has being for now. But "God is," the great truth and reality. And "I am," pure being untouched by the world. "It is; God is; I am." This was my chant, my song. I am surrounded by these dearest of friends. They encircled me, holding hands and chanting with me. *It is; God is; I am.*

I wait, and Grace comes. I did not even know I was at the High Meadow, but I was. Now I wait again, for this is the third day of the creation of my contemplative life. I wait, and the mind drifts. I observe it and gently center again on truth. If the challenge is greatly disturbing, I declare: *It is; God is; I am*, and wait again. Waiting is my way, but the fourth day is coming and waiting will have another companion with which to ponder and wonder.

To Catch A Bird

When I was a young boy, I decided to catch a bird. I acquired a large cardboard box and a forked stick. I attached a long string to the bottom of the stick and set an edge of the box in the fork of the stick. I placed bird food under the box. By tugging on the string, I could dislodge the stick and quickly bring the tilted box to the ground—capturing a bird in the upside-down box.

I waited. I focused, waiting for a bird. I persisted. If my attention wavered, I did not condemn myself. I gently brought my attention back to the task at hand. Eventually, a bird came, and my attention intensified. I pulled the string. I did it; I captured a bird only to release it, but I had a memory that over 60 years later helped me learn to wait at the High Meadow.

Summary

On the third day, I waited, and it is interesting that many of the revelations that came to me helped me learn to wait. Memories seen from new perspectives were more than remembrances. They lived in the moment and eased my discomfort and enabled me to wait and lose focus without self-condemnation and judgment. Catching a bird taught me focus and persistence. Leading campers up Mount Washington revealed where I was to wait—the High Meadow. Birds flying by our Lake of the Ozark cabin looked at me and smiled and eventually, I understood their message of outstretched wings. Even waiting for David at the airport showed me that waiting can be a delight. There was no need to berate myself when my attention strayed.

I discovered, as did the ancients, "Those who wait upon the Lord shall renew their strength: They shall mount up with wings like eagles…." (Isaiah 40:31). Those who wait for Grace gain strength, and waiting becomes a way of life—on the third day.

More provisions for the journey….

1. The High Meadow is an elevated state of *human* consciousness.
2. Affirmation and denial are processes of life that create states of consciousness of truth or error. Affirmation says yes and builds up. Denial says no and tears down. It also cleanses, purifies, and releases.
3. Affirmation and denial are spiritual practices that can take us to the High Meadow where we wait for Grace to take us higher.

4. We put on our wings and wait.
5. On the third day, the essence of my prayer practice was waiting.
6. The mind wanders when we wait.
7. As I waited and lost concentration, dear friends helped me. *It is; God is; I am.*
8. On the third day, I learned to wait; sometimes Grace came, and I stood on the summit of the mountain.

Waiting is a challenge; waiting opens doors, but there is more. Waiting invited Grace to join me, but Grace invited still another....

CHAPTER EIGHTEEN

A Prayerful Journey Continues
The Fourth Day

From Wandering To Wondering

The third day was a long day. My prayer practice—waiting at the High Meadow—lasted for years, and it changed my life. From time to time, Grace joined me, and I stood on the summit of the mountain and discovered the ever-expanding consciousness God is. Spiritual breakthroughs and revelations touched me and nudged me in new directions. Grace was an occasional visitor, but there was another presence that seemed to be a permanent resident of the High Meadow—the wandering mind.

In the last chapter, I told you of my relationship with this wanderer and the six words that helped me during my most tumultuous times while praying/meditating—*It is; God is, I am.* However, eventually another revelation eased the discontent I felt when my mind wandered.

I realized that the mind was not wandering; it was wondering. Sometimes it wondered about the state of the world, about my future or the fate of a friend or family member; sometimes it wondered what was for dinner. As I shifted from a wandering mind to a wondering mind, I became gentle with myself, and I saw more accurately my inner state of being. I saw what was moving in me. I no longer resisted the "wandering" mind. I was a curious watcher. I followed the wondering mind and learned what troubled it, what concerned it, what delighted it. A wandering mind is often frowned upon; a wondering mind is viewed with interest and compassion. I discovered this insight was an extension of a revelation of long ago—the sacred human.

The Sacred Human

The Sacred Human was one of the most important spiritual breakthroughs of my life. "Unless you accept your humanity, you won't be able to expression your divinity." I tried to push aside my humanity with its negative thoughts, feelings, and memories. I believed they did not support my new way of life, the positive, constructive Unity way of life, but then the scales fell from my eyes, and I saw that my humanity was sacred.

I was born of water and Spirit. I was human and divine. In fact, my humanity was just as sacred as my divinity because it was in the human arena where I learned to love.

Love's first act is acceptance, and I began to accept myself, my humanity, as it was and as it is. I did not try to change it or repair it. I accepted my foibles and mistakes and the thoughts, feelings and memories that came with them, and my true self took its first breath. I no longer wandered; I wondered. I was fully human, fully divine, fully alive.

The Fourth Day Dawns

It took more than four decades, but eventually I added love to my prayer practice. The wandering mind became the wondering mind, something to be observed like a young mother and father watching their newborn child. And I discovered I am not my mind. I am the one who watches and observes mind. I have a new name—the Watcher. However, the discovery of the wondering mind opened my heart; it led me to love. I added acceptance, love's first action, to my waiting.

On the fourth day, my prayer practice was more than putting on wings and climbing to the High Meadow. It was more than waiting and refocusing on an affirmation, denial, or breath. It was more than pondering a Bible story. It was more than sitting. It was loving. My new mantra was: As I wait, I love.

I discovered that the human condition with all its challenges was where I learned to love. I tried to love others, particularly those who irritated me, but I failed again and again. It was not until love joined waiting in prayer/meditation that I was able to truly love in the world. It seems so obvious: as within, so without. If I want to love my neighbor, I must first love and accept myself.

When I became still, what I needed to love and accept appeared. It did not emerge to make me miserable; it invited me to accept myself, to love myself. There was no longer resistance to the dark ore or darkness of my soul. I let it come, because it was my opportunity to love and accept all parts of myself, and to discover that love is essential to my reason for being.

Remember, as expressions of the EEC, the ever-expanding consciousness God is, we are curious; we are wonderers. We are also lovers. Through waiting, watching, and loving we accept all parts of ourselves. Then there is peace and contentment, each an invitation to Grace. Each a message to her that we are ready, that she can come to take us higher.

Many statements or ideas took their turn and attempted to center me as I waited at the High Meadow. "God is enough," "I am as God created me." "I am that I am." "My life is a prayer that God is praying." Now I added another, "As I wait, I love," and as I waited, watched and loved, I noticed something wonderful happening.

Attaining The Unattainable

The spiritual giants of ancient times exhibited extraordinary qualities of being: humility, meekness, non-resistance, strength, compassion, acceptance, and love. They went the extra mile, turned the other cheek, remained silent when falsely accused, and lived without condemnation. They attained what seemed unattainable to most human beings. They lived in the moment, and the moment was filled with God. They were patient and meek, and therefore they inherited the earth.

The spiritual giants are a puzzle to us. We don't understand how humility, a seemingly powerless state, can be filled with power. We shake our heads in disbelief when we are told to resist not evil. It seems impossible that the meek inherit the earth; they are fortunate to be able to have food to eat and water to drink. Love was Jesus' only commandment, and when the light of love passes through a prism of a spiritual giant, compassion and acceptance are witnessed in circumstances where most of us demand justice and punishment.

Father Henri Suso, a contemporary of Meister Eckhart, is an example of a spiritual giant. He lived in the 16th century in the Rhine Valley and was a member of a group called "friends of God" who wrote, circulated, read, and studied mystical writings.

A woman falsely accused this simple priest of fathering her child. Father Suso never denied her accusation, he never defended himself or condemned the woman. Many villagers and religious leaders condemned him. To complicate his situation, he helped to support and raise the child. A person who knew he had not fathered the child asked why he never denied or condemned the mother's accusations, and why did he compound matters by helping to raise the child. Father Suso answered, "Because the child needed my help."

How did Father Suso attain such qualities of being? I think it is because as he waited in prayer, he loved.

As I waited and loved, I noticed seemingly unattainable qualities of soul beginning to develop. I waited and learned how unruly the mind was, how uncentered and undisciplined I was, and it humbled me; however, being humbled does not insure humility. All of us are humbled. Our reaction to the humbling determines whether there will be humility.

Humility is a state of seeming powerlessness where true power resides. The humility principle states, "And whoever exalts himself will be humbled, but he who humbles himself will be exalted" (Matthew 23:12). Once we are humbled and on bended knee, one small "step" can be taken. "I of myself can do nothing." It is strange that a statement of powerlessness opens the door to the power God is.

For many years, before each Sunday service, I was alone with my thoughts and feelings. A statement of service, humility, and truth prepared me for each lesson and meditation I shared: *Here I am, Lord. Use me. I of myself can do nothing, through Christ I can do all things. I have the mind of the Christ. It is active in me now. I feel it. Where I stand You appear. When I speak, Your truth is heard, and Your love, peace and joy are felt.* I have never shared this preparatory practice until this moment.

Anyone who commits to a life of prayer/meditation encounters the wandering mind waiting to be known as the wondering mind. Anyone who prays/meditates is humbled and consequently is only a small step from humility and the discovery of true power. Those who humble themselves become meek, and the meek inherit the earth.

Pebble In The Pond

An inheritance does not come to us because of what we do; we inherit something because of our name, our nature, because of who and what we are. The meek know their true identity. They are expressions of the EEC, the ever-expanding consciousness God is.

They know true power, the power of consciousness, therefore they are not troubled and anxious when things are not yet manifest or when there is chaos and disorder. The meek understand that they have in their being the key to peace and contentment. They are the place where divine consciousness appears and its power is unleashed. The meek understand how manifestation works. This is why they can stand before Pilate and say nothing.

Consciousness manifests itself. It is like a pebble dropped in a pond. The pebble, the state of mind and heart, sends forth its ripples of manifestation into our lives and the cosmos. The meek know the nature of the ripples emanating from the pebble dropped in the cosmic pond.

When most people pray, they look to the world for a sign of answered prayer. They look into the manifest realm—a new job, a doctor's positive report, or a spouse who is willing to give marriage another chance. This is our human tendency, and it is the reason prayer is often undone.

The EEC, the Ever-Expanding Consciousness, cannot be seen; therefore, when the manifestation of a state of consciousness begins, it first appears in the unmanifest realm. The good news is that we have faculties of being that allow us to perceive the first signs that God is at work. The signs will be invisible, unknowable to our five senses, and yet we will know them.

Have you ever seen a feeling? Feelings cannot be seen, but they can bring us to our knees or lift us up. Often, answered prayer begins as a feeling of peace or contentment in a situation where there should be no peace. Let us be sensitive to spiritual consciousness moving in the unseen realms that we can recognize.

Have you ever seen an idea or a thought? Ideas and thoughts are invisible, unknown to our senses, but they can be perceived. The beginning of all things is an idea. Often the revelation of God is through ideas and thoughts. Look for them. Take your eyes off the world. Don't judge by appearances. Develop sensitivity to the unseen realm in which consciousness is first made manifest. Feelings, thoughts, and ideas are some of the first ripples in the pond.

The meek inherit the earth (the realm of manifestation) because they know how things come into being and are sensitive to the subtle activity of God in our lives.

Another possible first sign of answered prayer is an image that comes through a dream or vision. Many people are guided by images. Dreams, visions, and images have no tangible substance, but their message can guide us, lift us, and bolster our faith.

Feelings, thoughts, ideas, dreams, visions, and images are the first signs that consciousness is being made manifest. The meek know this. The first signs are the beginning of inheriting the world. Things and situations come into manifestation because of who the meek are, because of the state of their being.

The first signs are in the faculties of thinking, feeling, and imagination. The next sign witnessed by those who know and understand the dynamics of manifestation is in the physical body. This is where healing takes place. There is a movement from the unseen to the seen, from the intangible state of wholeness and life to the tangible state of the body. Each of our faculties and the corresponding manifestation are like ripples created by a pebble dropped into a pond. The pebble is the spiritual state of consciousness or revelation we experience as pure Silence. Then the manifestation begins, but the first concentric circles are within us: feelings, thoughts, ideas, dreams, visions, and images, and then spiritual consciousness touches flesh and blood. Tears may flow, energy may move up the spine, spontaneous healings can occur or a slow, orderly restoration of health may begin.

More rings emanate as the pebble touches our physical world. Jobs are offered, relationships form or healings occur. Opportunities are presented and recognized. This is the wonder of divine revelation or inheritance; it comes with the ability to recognize the opportunity. Opportunities often come, but they pass us by; they are not recognized. The meek have eyes to see. They know manifestation when it begins. The meek know what to look for and where to look.

I waited and loved and was humbled. I acknowledged my lack of personal power and found humility. I saw the power of meekness and why the meek inherit the earth. What comes to them is the result of their awareness of the ever-expanding consciousness God is. This is why they do not fear failure or the posturing of those who think they are powerful. They know true power, and that it is their responsibility to awaken to EEC.

The qualities of the soul we most revere and strive for are never born in the world. They are first experienced in silence as we wait and love. Prayer/meditation humbles us, but it is where we discover humility. We seek power in the world through money and position and through the use of our word, but power comes not when we speak, but when we hear the Word spoken. The voice of revelation, the voice still and small, speaks, and there is light. Another pebble enters the pond, but it did not drop from our hand.

The Extra Mile

When confronted with injustice most of us want to fight. We resist and confront the tyranny. We want to destroy the corruption we see or experience. The spiritual giants follow a different path. They are true to their nature and seek not to destroy, but to illumine.

Consider this...You are a Jew standing in a crowd as a squad of Roman soldiers marches through your village. A soldier stops and scans the crowd. His eyes fall on you. "You, Jew, come here." You reluctantly walk toward him.

He hands you his shield. "You will carry my burden." You know the law. Any Roman can compel a Jew to carry his load for one mile. You walk behind the soldier, and he looks over his shoulder at you, a smirk on his face. He smiles. He sees your face flushed red, not with the heat of the Palestine sun, but with rage and anger. He thinks he is the conqueror, and you are the conquered.

After walking a mile, the soldier looks for another person to carry his shield. In that moment you remember the words of the teacher of Nazareth, who said, "And whoever compels you to go one mile, go with him two" (Matthew 5:41).

You say, "Roman, may I carry your burden another mile?"

The soldier turns. "What?" You repeat your request. He nods and pulls back to walk next to you. He looks at you, and you look at him. You walk together, no longer conqueror and conquered, but two men walking side-by-side.

Those who walk the extra mile know themselves and the true nature of the unkind, corrupt, and unjust. They know true power. They are the meek who inherit the earth, but they don't want to live in the world alone. They gather to themselves others willing to discover their true nature.

Resist Not

One of the most puzzling and seemingly unrealistic statements ever spoken was: "Resist not evil." Few people have ever put this principle to the test. Instead, we think evil must be resisted, confronted, and destroyed. A holocaust cannot continue or be repeated. Evil must be overcome.

Silence has taught me that how I want to live in the world must first live in me. Non-resistance in the world must first be practiced in prayer/meditation. The regrets and guilt and shame I would push aside or destroy, the thoughts and feelings and memories I would resist, must be brought into the light. I need to hear their story rather than turn a deaf ear to what they say. I need to hear them, rather than resist them.

Like all things, non-resistance begins in me; then and only then do I have the insight to apply it in the world. It is not an accident that those who have put this principle to the test are those who fully embraced their humanity and who practiced the art of waiting and loving. The great qualities of soul support one another: non-resistance, turning the other cheek, meekness, acceptance, and love. They are spiritual qualities and practices whose power is first discovered when we are still. We yearn for God, but it is ourselves we first encounter; and this encounter humbles us and asks us to resist not, turn the other cheek, trust the power of meekness and practice love and acceptance.

Odd, isn't it? We pray/meditate and our first encounter is not God; it is ourselves, and the encounter humbles us, making us candidates for humility and meekness. Our humanity reaches out to us and silently mouths what it wants—acceptance and love. Persistence takes the place of resistance, and eventually we make peace with our humanity. Our water birth is complete, and our spiritual birth continues.

Strength

One of the first soul qualities to emerge and grow when we pray/meditate is strength, our ability to persist and endure. For most of us, our contemplative life is a cycle of starts and stops. We are enthusiastic, but then we think we are incompetent or unsuited for a contemplative life. Our humanity becomes evident and because of it, we believe we cannot pray/meditate. We quit, only to begin again, and with every new beginning, we grow stronger.

Strength, the ability to persist, is necessary for the achievement of any goal. It is one of the first faculties of being to develop. Consider the following: a person engages in a contemplative practice and has a wonderful spiritual experience, and the next day he is eager to sit again. He longs for a similar experience. Another person waits, and the experience is chaos. The mind is a rover and the contemplative time is clouded with memories and remembered feelings and thoughts. The next day, she waits again.

Strength is growing in the second person because it takes persistence to wait again when there is inner turmoil. Anyone can return to waiting when the previous experience was positive. Only those who wait and watch when there is chaos and seeming failure grow stronger.

Persistence Leads to Patience

The High Meadow is a gathering place. The wandering mind resides there, but eventually this inhabitant is given a new name—wonderer. The past and future also inhabit the High Meadow. We wait and regrets join us. Guilt and shame appear. Sometimes the past gives way to future dreams and fears. Doubt often joins the conversation, and our confidence is eroded. The past and the future obscure our vision and ability to see the one true inhabitant of the High Meadow, the present moment.

Only when we wait and love and cease our resistance of the past and future do we experience the power of now. Now is more than a moment in time; it is a gateway to the kingdom of God; it is our connection to all that God is.

When the past and future dominate us, we are powerless. We are powerless because the past no longer exists, and the future is yet to be. Either state of consciousness can have power over us, but they do not connect us to the power of the Ever-Expanding Consciousness. However, if we choose to dwell in the powerless states of past and future, all is not lost. They can introduce us to another powerless state—humility. This is a strange place, for although we feel powerless when we are humbled, the experience of divine power is near.

The spiritual path is sinuous; there are detours, but the spiritual path always leads back to the ever-expanding consciousness God is.

Even the powerless states of past and future take us home because they point to humility. Any powerless state can do this sacred work, for the powerlessness of humility is the path to power, just as meekness reveals the power of consciousness and its natural propensity to manifest itself.

Powerless human states of consciousness always humble us, but it is possible to avoid the detours of past, future, and resistance. Something as simple as the present moment waits for us to wait and love.

Now, The Gateway To The Kingdom

Our senses, our breath, can take us into the moment. The moment may appear empty, but it is full of all that is needed. People who dwell in the past or future are impatient and powerless. Those who dwell in the moment are patient and powerful, for an experience of the moment is a consciousness of connection.

Years ago, I wrote a script entitled, "A Closer Walk With God" to be used at spiritual retreats. The script invites retreatants into the moment where they meet the Ever-Expanding Consciousness.

The closer walk begins in a meeting space where I explain the upcoming walk with God. As each person leaves the gathering space, he receives an envelope with the first installment of the script for an hour-long walk in silence. The retreatant opens the envelope and reads the script. It outlines a series of practices that engage four of their five senses: sight, sound, touch and smell.

The wonderful thing about our senses is that they bring us into the moment. They know nothing of the past or future. The retreatants notice light and shadow, shapes near and far. They listen for sounds close and distant, loud noises and whispers, chirps of birds and the whisper of the wind. They take off their shoes and walk in the cool grass and feel their feet touch the ground. They sit in silence with their eyes open and closed. They smell flowers. They hug trees and touch leaves and the pedals of flowers. They observe critters and allow the tiniest insect its rite of passage. As they walk, they are instructed to look for an object that speaks to them, an object to bring back to the room where the walk began.

At the end of the hour, the retreatants return to the room where they started, and I greet them with a hug and another envelope with their final instructions. Soft music adds to the sacredness of the moment. Their silence continues as they place their object on a long piece of craft paper that stretches twenty or thirty feet across the floor. The instructions in the second envelope ask them to describe their experience by drawing or writing on the paper with markers, pens, and pencils that are provided.

Finally, the silence is broken as each retreatant talks briefly about their closer walk with God. They read what they wrote, their statements or their poems. They explain their pictures or mandalas. I have never been at a retreat where there were not tears from some of the people who walked with God.

What happens is that the senses bring us into the moment, and the moment is a meeting place where God is real. It moves us. I remember a retreat where there was a man who seemed distracted as I explained the closer walk with God, but when he returned from his walk and hugged me, he broke down and cried. I held him for five minutes as his chest rose and fell, as he sobbed for joy and overflowed with the Presence. It is a privilege beyond words to hold someone who is overflowing with God. I said to him, "I see you found God on your walk."

Summary

While we wait and love, we may fail, but we persist and grow stronger and eventually view our "failure" differently. Our wandering mind humbles us, and we feel powerless, but this is the path to humility. The past and future assault us, but we do not resist.

We wait and love and live in the moment and become patient. We do not resist thoughts, feelings, memories, or images of the mind. Each simply is…God is and I am. We turn the other cheek. We accept what is, and love our humanity. We are meek because we discover that it is only through consciousness that things and life come into being.

More provisions for the journey….

1. On the fourth day of the creation of my contemplative life I waited. I loved.
2. As I waited and loved, I noticed extraordinary qualities of being emerging from within me: humility, meekness, non-resistance, compassion, love, and acceptance.
3. Humility is a seemingly powerless state that leads to all power.
4. The meek understand the power of consciousness and how manifestation works.
5. Answered prayer begins not in the world, but within us as thoughts, ideas, feelings, dreams, visions, or images. Then the pebble dropped in the pond manifests itself in the body and in our life circumstances and experiences.
6. The permanent resident of the High Meadow is the present moment, the gateway to the kingdom of God. To dwell in the moment is to know patience and that *now* is a connection to the power of the ever-expanding consciousness God is.
7. All powerless states such as the past, future, and being humbled lead to the power of the ever-expanding consciousness God is.

Come with me. Another day is dawning. Let us practice the Presence.

CHAPTER NINETEEN

A Prayerful Journey Continues
The Fifth Day

A Dawning

On the fifth day, there comes a dawning, a revelation. If we can experience the ever-expanding consciousness God is for a few moments, we must be able to experience the Presence momently, to be continually aware of the First Light. For most of us, the spiritual journey is like walking in a garden and inhaling the fragrance of the blossoms. When the air is still, the fragrance of the flowers is known, but when a breeze moves through the garden, the fragrance fades. As mature practitioners of spirituality, we often sense the Presence when we are still, but when the air moves, when we are in the midst of life and its challenges, the awareness fades; our consciousness shifts from the interior to the exterior, from spiritual things to added things.

Is this the spiritual life? The touch of the Divine, a gentle nudge, the brush of angel's wings and then nothing? We are left not with an experience, but with a longing to walk with God rather than to feel from time to time a gentle touch on our cheek or the excitement and possibilities of a new revelation. Is it not possible to live continuously in an awareness of God? To know that the First Light is part of every thought and feeling, dream and vision, to know it is divine power that enables us to kneel and pick up a glistening stone from a mountain stream.

The Celts of ancient times asked similar questions and sought a way to live perpetually aware of God. They conceived prayers for nearly every task—for milking cows, churning butter, for planting, and for harvesting, for washing and eating. They knew God was with them, and these spiritual seekers sought a way to live in conscious oneness with the One; they looked for a way for God to be a part of everything they did. At the center of their lives was the Apostle Paul's call written in a letter to the Thessalonians—pray constantly.

My Dawning

I felt the dawning. I followed the logic. If it is possible to experience the ever-expanding consciousness God is once, it must be possible to experience this consciousness continuously.

God has many names: El Shaddai, God of the mountain, Adonai, Lord, or Elohim. Some think the name of God is unspeakable. To name a thing gives it form, and God is formless. Others insist God is love. The Creator named Itself *I am that I am*, and declared Its nature is pure being, pure consciousness.

Jesus, the heretical Jew, felt God's closeness and called the Hebrew deity Father. This was a revelation to His followers because they believed God was set apart in the Holy of Holies in the Temple. Only the High Priest entered this room once a year on the Day of Atonement. Jesus' God was like a father, close and personal.

I, too, looked for a name that conveyed closeness, and for many years I, like Abraham, called God Friend. I still do, but now I have another name for God, the EEC, the Ever-Expanding Consciousness that was and is the First Light. I know it is strange; I know it is heretical, but I like it. It is consistent with the Creator's name for Itself—*I am that I am*. This is a declaration of pure consciousness. It is the image and likeness in which I am made, for I am consciousness, ideally an ever-expanding consciousness filled with wonder and curiosity—like a child.

I have a desire, a yearning, to pray without ceasing. I desire to be continuously aware of the First Light. For many years, this was my quest, and I failed miserably. Although the yearning was and is part of my spiritual quest, the failure was and is a part of my human experience. The failure helped me understand the sacred human.

Following The Mystics

Earlier I mentioned the lives and writings of the mystics and how they gutted my soul and transformed me. Nothing was more inspiring than reading about their quest to pray constantly. Nicolas Herman, born in 1611, became a soldier and then a footman, but at age fifty-five, he entered the Carmelite order and took the name Brother Lawrence. He worked in an infirmary kitchen until his death in 1691at age eighty. During these years, he became known for his "practice of the presence of God." This simple monk advised people of all walks of life about perpetual prayer, even church leaders. A year after his death, sixteen letters and four conversations about his prayer practice were published.

Brother Lawrence was often alone, but he did nothing alone. His actions and activities were dedicated to God. It brought him peace, and people noticed his sense of the Presence. Eventually, he gave little credence to daily prayer practices because he lived perpetually in a consciousness of the First Light. His daily tasks were not less than his daily devotions. God was real and a part of everything he did, and everything he did, he did for God.

Brother Lawrence continually talked to God. He wrote, "My prayers are nothing other than a sense of the presence of God." His life emerged from a single quest, "I began to live as if there were nothing, absolutely nothing but Him. I kept my mind in his holy presence." The result was: "...joys so continual and so great I can scarce contain them."

In his last letter written on February 6, 1691, he wrote, "Oh, dear friend, the Lord is not outside of you, pouring down favors. The Lord is within you. Seek Him there, within...and nowhere else." These final words continue to be an inspiration to practice the Presence.

Over 300 years later, Frank Laubach, who was born in the United States on September 2, 1884, embarked upon the same quest. At age forty-five while serving as a missionary in Mindanao, Philippines, he began to pray constantly. It was an experiment that continued until his death on June 11, 1970.

On June 23, 1930, he wrote: "One question now to be put to the test is this: Can we have that contact with God all the time? All the time awake, fall asleep in His arms, and awaken in His presence? Can we attain that? Can we do His will all the time? Can we think His thoughts all the time?"

Frank Laubach lived in a tiny hut on Signal Hill, Philippines. He wondered if he could bring to mind a thought of God once every minute. He knew he could not see God, but he thought of God playfully hiding behind every rock and tree. Like Brother Lawrence, he brought God into every task. He wondered if he could sense God controlling his hands as he shaved or dressed or ate breakfast. As the experiment progressed, He wrote that the practice was strenuous, but his earthly tasks ceased being laborious.

He kept a diary of his experiment. On June 1, 1930, he wondered, "Do you suppose that through all eternity the price we will need to pay for keeping God will be that we must endlessly be giving Him away."

Frank Laubach's diary excerpts are some of the most inspirational words I ever read. "The most important discovery of my whole life is that one can take a little rough cabin and transform it into a palace just by flooding it with God."

Nancy and I live in a cabin in the North Georgia mountains. I wonder if one day we will perceive it to be a palace.

There were no distractions for Mr. Laubach. On September 18, 1931, he wrote this diary entry, "I choose to look at people through God, using God as my glasses, colored with His love for them." Frank Laubach's writings inspired me, challenged me and frustrated me because where he succeeded, I failed, but at least I had multiple opportunities to accept myself as I am and wonder how I could practice the presence.

I read a spiritual classic, *The Way of the Pilgrim*, written by an anonymous Russian pilgrim who practiced the Presence. His method was different from Brother Lawrence and Frank Laubach. He memorized a statement that many Christians resonate with, "Lord Jesus Christ, have mercy on me." The book follows his travels and adventures as he informs fellow seekers about his attempt to wed the statement, "Lord Jesus Christ, have mercy on me," to his walking, to his breath, and even to his heartbeat. The idea was that eventually his constant breath and ceaseless beating heart rhythmically prayed the prayer.

The Russian pilgrim began by verbally declaring the prayer hundreds and then thousands of times a day. He spoke the words out loud; he held the words in mind. As he walked, he wed the words to his steps, to his breath and to his heart beat, so eventually he did not have to speak the words of his prayer. His breath prayed the prayer. His heart beat formed the words "Lord Jesus Christ, have mercy on me."

My First Attempts

My first attempt at practicing the Presence followed Frank Laubach's quest to remember God once an hour with the goal of thinking of God once a minute. I set an alarm on my watch to help me remember, but the world is louder than any alarm. I became involved with work, family, friends and fun, trauma and chaos, and I forgot. It was humbling to go hours without thinking of God for even a moment. I tried and failed and tried again.

I slowed my movements in an attempt to perceive the power that made the movement possible. I bathed and pondered water baptism and its cleansing power. I ate and thought of the prophet fed by the ravens and the manna that fed the Hebrews wandering in the wilderness. I was one of the 5,000 people Jesus fed with five loaves and two fish. I watched the breaking of the bread and the blessing of the drink during the last supper.

I integrated silence into everything I did. Before every meeting, I sat in silence with people I counseled and at board and staff meetings. Before every difficult task, I declared, "I of myself can do nothing; through Christ I can do all things." I paused and listened and looked to see if I could "see" the Presence.

I once wrote of a make-believe culture that taught their children that God was always with them, and if the children looked quickly over their left shoulder, they could catch a glimpse of their Creator. I looked over my left shoulder and saw nothing, but my willingness to look helped me remember I am not alone.

I walked and wed different statements to my movements and breath. "I and the Father are one." "My God, my all, I love you." These rhythmic seven-syllable mantras were in step with my steps and my breath. I used many different statements, but in most instances, they consisted of seven syllables. Let me tell you why I used seven-syllable phrases and statements.

The Rhythm of Seven

After working at Unity's world headquarters for twelve years, I was asked to create a series of courses for the Continuing Education

Program of Unity School of Religious Studies. One of the courses was entitled, "The Spiritual Journey." It takes the student on a journey exploring his or her human and spiritual experiences.

I posed a question in the first class. "When did your spiritual journey begin?" Most people thought of a significant spiritual event or when they became a member of their church; however, the truth is that they are spiritual beings, and therefore they have always been on a spiritual journey whether they are conscious of it or not. The class helped the students discover the subtle spiritual undertones of their lives.

The student notes their physical birth, but also searches for times of spiritual awakening. Triumphs and tragedies are reviewed as well as detours and crossroads and breakthroughs. Miracles and wonders are acknowledged as well as altars and sacred places and events. Also, rites of passage are explored: Moving from being Problem Oriented to Solution Oriented to God Oriented. Other interesting passages are: Never Mind to Take Thought to Take No Thought; Out of Control, In Control to Surrender; Victim, Master, Servant; It Happens to Me, I Make It Happen, I Let it Happen; and Traditional to Metaphysical to Mystical. Some of these passages are unknown to the student, but they lie ahead. Some students are stuck in a passage and need a nudge to take the next step. The class and its fellowship encourage and challenge students to progress to the next rite of passage.

The journaling, discoveries, and classroom practices lead to two life-changing and illuminating exercises. The first is the creation of a Life Chart. The chart is a pictorial representation of the student's life journey. I have witnessed many forms through the years, but they all contain the ingredients of a spiritual life, ranging from birth to breakthroughs, from detours and crossroads to wonders and miracles, altars and sacred places as well as triumphs and tragedies. Each student has the opportunity to present his or her life chart to a small group of fellow students and to talk about key breakthroughs and experiences and new insights discovered as a result of the class.

The second exercise promotes a conscious spiritual journey and the healing of past hurts as well as providing provisions for a continuing spiritual journey.

Attention is given to unresolved or hurtful situations, conditions and experiences revealed through the class exercises. The students become still and wait for seven-syllable statements to rise out of areas of their lives that need healing, resolution, or insight. Examples are: I and the Father Are One, Filled With the Grandeur of God, Be Still and Know I Am God or Healed, Restored, Cherished, and Loved. Once the seven-syllable phrase or statement emerges, it becomes a special friend that leads the individual to greater revelations and healing.

The wonder of the spiritual journey class is that the source for the phrases and statements is our lives. I love seven syllables because in most instances they are rhythmic and can be sung or intoned or wed to the cadence of our steps or breath or even heartbeat. They help us remember our quest to practice the Presence.

Monks Of The Mountain

During the writing of this chapter of *An Autobiography of a Christian Heretic*, I renewed my quest to be continually aware of the EEC. I have a new insight into the failure that has plagued me as I responded to Paul's call to pray constantly. I now know that I failed because I thought I could succeed. Personal success seems fundamental to so many human endeavors, but in spirituality failure is personal; it is ours, but success is transcendent of us. Success is the work of the Ever-Expanding Consciousness God. This revelation lifted me. It is fresh—just a few days old as I am writing to you. It is freeing to know that the failure is mine, but the success is transcendent of self. This realization encourages me. I feel relief and an eagerness to go forward as I never have before.

I am adding a new focus to my prayer/meditation time—a willingness to discover new practices that help me know and experience the consciousness in which I dwell and which is the truth of my being.

I began this practice on July 7, 2021, and I have a number of new practices to put to the test. They are questions to pose to the Ever-Expanding Consciousness. "What do you see?" What do you hear? What do you say about… this person, situation, thing?" In addition, when I looked at my schedule book today, I felt guided to write at the beginning of each day—Remember. Remember to practice the Presence. I have a feeling that as I write "Remember" at the beginning of each day what I am to remember will change. Today I write Remember. Perhaps tomorrow I will write, Remember, you are not alone. Remember to breathe. Remember to wait. Remember to listen. Remember… Perhaps, a spiritual life is a life of remembering, not a look at the past, but a reminder of what is at hand. I am sure Jesus would ask me and all humankind to remember that the kingdom of heaven is at hand.

I now cherish monastic moments. I pause and do nothing, say nothing, read nothing. I simply pause and remember; I remember an affirmation, a special friend, a story, a person. I remember to wait for a revelation….

Recently, I asked God, "What are you doing?" The first time I asked, the EEC answered, "Wondering." The second time I asked, this answer came: "What I am always doing." Later I remember God is being, exploring, discovering what works in this universe and what does not work, awakening. God is not simply being; God is becoming, becoming continually individualized as you and me. And what are we doing? We are becoming increasingly aware.

My various practices of perpetual prayer reveal I am becoming an invisible man, so that where I stand, the Ever-Expanding-Consciousness appears and that when I speak, the Truth is heard, the First Light shines, and love, peace, and joy are felt.

And so I begin again in this simple way, a monk of the mountain, more keenly aware of my surroundings, people, creatures, thoughts, feelings, images and discoveries; more a child than I have ever been, filled with wonder and curiosity. Not wondering about tomorrow, but wondering about the fullness of the moment. There is so much to remember.

More provisions for the journey….

1. If we can be aware of God for a few moments, we can be conscious of the EEC continually. This quest is an answer to Paul's call to pray constantly.
2. Prayer practices aligned to the practice of the Presence range from prayers wed to daily activity, to the perpetual praying of a particular prayer to wedding prayerful thoughts and the cadence of our steps, our breathing or our heartbeat.
3. The practice of the Presence includes continual conversations with God and pausing to sense the divine power behind our simplest movements.
4. Part of the joy and the challenge of praying without ceasing is opening ourselves to new prayer practices that expand our consciousness, so we are aware of the ever-expanding consciousness God is.
5. If we choose to practice the Presence, let us remember we are not alone.

Come with me. There is another day in the creation of my contemplative live, a day in which my life became a life that God is praying.

CHAPTER TWENTY

A Prayerful Journey Continues
The Six Day

The High Meadow

One of the most beautiful places we ever lived was Sunrise Beach, Missouri. Our house was built in stages. The first was a thousand square foot frame house sitting eighty feet above Lake of the Ozark. We faced west and looked down two arms of a river that became a lake in 1931 when the Army Corp of Engineers completed Bagnell Dam and created a sinuous body of water that snaked its way through hills and bluffs created by the meandering Osage River. To our south was a 200-foot cliff that caught the westerly winds and created the updraft that carried birds of prey to soaring heights. It was these winds and birds that planted the seed for "put on your wings," one of the meditative practices that lifts me in consciousness.

The second phase of our lake home was a second-floor master bedroom suite and study as well as a garage. Later a sunroom was built on the lake side of the house. We named our home the High Meadow. A local artist created a sign depicting a meadow with colorful flowers and evergreen trees. The name came from my experience on the Appalachian Trial at an approach to the summit of Mount Washington in New Hampshire. I shared this experience in Chapter 17. It is amazing that youthful experiences bear fruit later in life, for the mountain chalet cabin where we currently live is marked by a sign created by Nancy—High Meadow II. As guests climb the driveway and near the front door, two signs greet them—Practice the Presence and A Place to Awaken.

The first High Meadow was an alluring place. One weekend, Bill and Marge Dale, friends from Unity Village, visited us. We woke up on a rainy Saturday morning, and Marge and Bill met a Realtor to look at some property. We were assured, "We're just looking." Several hours later, our drenched friends returned. Marge looked shocked, her eyes wide as if trying to take in what happened. Bill was grinning from ear to ear. He said, "We put an option on two lots on the lake." Indeed, the High Meadow was an alluring place. Bill and Marge later built a beautiful home high on a bluff not far from our home.

Friends of God Unity Church

When we left Unity Village, we moved to the High Meadow in Sunrise Beach. It felt like a state of retirement, a place to pause, but we didn't rest long. We had pioneered a ministry in Raleigh, North Carolina and thought of pioneering a church in Sunrise Beach, but the community had a recorded population of 262 people. While working at Unity Village, I met two new friends, Helen Purvis and her daughter, Kathy Tankersley, who were attending a retreat. They lived not far from our lake home. We talked about starting a Unity work in the area. Later, I learned of other Unity people who lived in the area or who were at the lake part of the year: Jan Lee, Judy and Harold Haines, and Linda and Dale Froling. I taught several classes open to the public at a community room at a local bank and created a call-in phone line with positive, helpful, practical messages. These were the seeds of what was to come.

We invited several people to our home to talk about the possibility of starting a Unity work. By the time the meeting was over, we selected a date for the first service and assigned tasks to individuals to find a place to meet and to acquire a sound system. At the meeting, I took a penny and blessed it. I then asked those present to hold the penny and give their blessing. The coin was returned to me. Taking a page from Charles and Myrtle's playbook, I informed the group that the penny was the total assets of the newly emerging ministry and that we were going to give it away, that our beginning would be generosity and that we were totally dependent on God.

After everyone left, Nancy, who was looking forward to six months of rest after our work at Unity Village, said to me, "What the hell just happened here?"

I said, "I guess we are pioneering again."

The High Meadow, Our Home

While we worked at Unity's world headquarters at Unity Village, we spent many weekends at the High Meadow. I ached when we left on Sunday, I loved it so much. The peace at the High Meadow was like standing at Monticello Lawn near the summit of Mount Washington, feeling the wind and gazing sixty miles into the distance. The serenity encompassed my whole world.

We did pioneer a Unity ministry at Lake of the Ozarks, Friends of God Unity Church, and we built a three-story observatory rising above our house. It housed a 14" telescope controlled by a computer in a climate-controlled room on the first floor. I remember the dedication and ribbon-cutting star party for the High Meadow Observatory. We served "planetary punch" as well as moon pies, Milky Way bars and star fruit. People stood in line late into the night to see the wonders of the heaven. I was on the observation deck with our guests speaking to Nancy in the control room through a headset. Planets, galaxies, and globular clusters came into focus, accompanied by sounds of wonder and awe.

At the High Meadow, I recovered from the kidney donation. At the High Meadow my mother christened the USS Ocracoke, a 14-foot cosine wherry rowboat I built, and at the High Meadow I wrote, *The Prayer That God Prays.*

The rowboat and the book were intertwined. The USS Ocracoke was made of thin strips of cedar with oak gunnels and a mahogany transom and bowsprit. The oars were sitka spruce, hand-made and covered with leather where they rested in the oar locks. Harold Haynes and I started the project in his garage, and eventually we moved the project to my garage, and over the course of several years I completed it.

The boat was made waterproof by layers of fiberglass, epoxy and varnish. The many layers below the waterline were sanded, creating clouds of fiberglass, sawdust and varnish particulates. The result was not only a boat, but a massive sinus infection. The infection lasted for six months. During that time, I only slept a few hours at a time. I was up at night running on a tread mill—so I could breathe. It was agony.

The Prayer That God Prays

Since I was awake in the middle of the night, I decided to write a book, *The Prayer That God Prays.* The idea of God praying came to me many years before. During a time of prayer/meditation while in Spokane, Washington, the still, small voice whispered in my ear. "Your life is a prayer that I am praying."

I was confused. God didn't pray, and my life certainly was not a prayer and definitely not God's prayer. I never forgot the experience. It was a revelation, but it was not enlightening. It was confusing until I started to write the book. Clarity came in two ways. Amazingly, when I wrote, it was as if there was no infection. I breathed easily. When I became tired and went to bed, the agony of restricted breathing and intense sinus pressure returned. Night after night, this cycle of clarity and agony returned, but during the times of clarity, the book was written.

The Prayer That God Prays is a tiny book that was written in a few months, but it contains interesting insights that join together to explain how my life, anyone's life, can be God's prayer.

First, there must be a new definition, a new understanding of what prayer is. Prayer is an experience of God's presence. There are many prayer practices, but prayer is an experience, an experience of the ever-expanding consciousness God is. Second, the revelation of the EEC does not come into being through my efforts. I have my work to do to rise to the High Meadow, but the experience comes through Grace. In other words, the experience is "God's doing." Third, my life and in fact all of our lives are destined to flow from a consciousness of the First Light, the Ever-Expanding Consciousness.

This is another aspect of consciousness. Not only do we see through our consciousness as if it is an eye or window, it is where our actions and our lives originate. Often the way we live flows from a consciousness of error and fear, but there is always the possibility for our lives to flow from a divine source, a "fountainhead high in the mountains."

I now understood. If my life flowed from a consciousness of the ever-expanding consciousness God is, and if that dawning of awareness came into being through the activity of God, my life would be God's prayer, not my own.

The words echoed from the past—your life is a prayer that I am praying. At this point in my life, my quest was to be constantly aware of the presence of God and to live from this consciousness. Since the dawning of this awareness came through Grace, and since prayer is an experience of the Presence, my life could be God's prayer. My life was not solely my own, it was an expression of the EEC; it was God's prayer. This I now believe is the destiny for each of us.

The book was published, and I often center myself with the words, "My life is a prayer that God is praying." I loved the feel of the words. They flowed like a song. I loved their rhythm, their cadence. Pause and say the words out loud and feel their harmony. They dance to the music of the spheres.

While attending a conference, I spied two friends, two song writers sitting at a table in the restaurant where Nancy and I were eating. I scribbled, "My life is a prayer that God is praying" on a napkin and approached Stowe Daily and Karen Taylor Good. I told them a little about the statement and that I thought it might be a foundation for a song. I left the napkin with them.

A couple of hours later, we received a call from Karen and Stowe, asking us to come to their room. They had a surprise for us. Nancy and I rushed to their room and sat across the bed from them as they sang, "My Life Is a Prayer," a song that was nominated for a New Thought Posi Award. Nancy and I cried.

When I look back at the days of the creation of my contemplative life, the revelation *your life is a prayer that I am praying,* carries a message that will feed me throughout eternity. My life, like all life, is destined to flow from the ever-expanding consciousness God is.

I progressed from trying to get God to act and fulfill my needs to transforming my consciousness through spiritual practices, so needs could be fulfilled. My affirmative prayer practice was filled with many words, but when I began to hold the words in my mind and rest with them, waiting broke through as the dawn of the third day of the creation of my prayer life. Then love and practicing the Presence enlivened me and awakened me to the realization of many years ago: My life is a prayer that God is praying.

The Squirrel and the Bear

Nancy and I hiked in the shadow of the Grand Tetons at Colter Bay on a peninsula jutting out into Jackson Lake. A ranger told us to be alert because a bear and her cubs were in the area. Carrying our bear spray, we noisily hiked the shore of the lake. We came to a bend in the trail and in front of us was a squirrel. He stood on his hind legs in the middle of the path. He was jabbering and chirping. He refused to move from the center of the trail.

After a minute he dashed into the forest. Mystified, we continued our hike. After 75 yards I smelled a beastly odor. I told Nancy and we hurried along the trail.

I believe the squirrel knew of the presence of the bear and her cubs and his jabbering was a warning to us. The little creature either saved us from emotional trauma, bodily harm, or worse.

Life is meant to be God's prayer. Life flows from our consciousness. Ideally, our experiences are born out of the First Light. This is what happened on the path at Colter Bay, and our experience of the Presence called for a squirrel to assist two hikers experiencing the beauty and wonder of the Grand Tetons.

Prayer/meditation is not *about* life; it *is* life. To be alive is to be aware, and to truly live is to be aware of the ever-expanding consciousness God is. All we think, feel, imagine, say, do, and experience is destined to originate in God. This is the loftiest of goals; it is a desire planted in us that fills us with wonder, and wonder and desire are evidence of the Ever-Expanding Consciousness.

This may seem impossible, but the truth is we live from our consciousness. What if the life we live came not from human consciousness with all its foibles and error? What if our lives flowed from a consciousness of the First Light?

More provisions for the journey….

1. Prayer is a consciousness of God.
2. The experience of this Ever-Expanding Consciousness does not come through our efforts. It comes through Grace.
3. Prayer, the experience of the Presence, is something God "does."

4. Human experience flows from consciousness; life as it is meant to be flows from the ever-expanding consciousness God is.
5. My life is a prayer that God is praying. Yours can be, too.

You, dear friend, have lived with me through my explanation of the six days of the creation of my contemplative life. I am sure more days will follow, but for now I am content. Perhaps the seventh day is simply a day of rest when nothing needs to happen other than the living of life.

Come with me as we discover heresy is the way.

CHAPTER TWENTY-ONE

When Heresy Becomes The Way

Heresy Is A Question of Authority

What was the most astonishing thing about Jesus? Was it walking on water or changing water to wine? For the sick, it was healing. For the hungry, it was the multiplication of bread and fish. For traditional Christians, it was Jesus' resurrection, His return from the dead, the cornerstone of their faith. However, the scripture says what astonished people was Jesus spoke with His own authority. "And they were astonished at His teaching, for He taught them as one having authority, and not as the scribes" (Mark 1:22).

Most religions begin with someone's encounter with God. The individual's consciousness is elevated, which invites more experiences, revelations, and insights. The founder shares a new perspective, a promising way of life, and attracts disciples. The life and teachings of the founder are recorded. A religion is born. The history of the life and teachings of the founder become the authority for future generations and their actions. This authority is rooted in the past. It draws life from the founder's encounter with the consciousness God is. The encounter is revered, but its significance is forgotten. The true authority and power are not the religion or its sacred book; its authority is a spiritual experience.

Jesus' authority wasn't Judaism or the Law and the Prophets. It was His personal experience with God. He knew the One of whom He spoke. The people sensed this, but they failed to understand that Jesus called them to the same path, to personal revelation. In the mind of some, this is the birth of heresy because the authority is not the religion, its sacred book or its clergy; the authority is a person's experience with God.

On Whose Authority?

The content of *An Autobiography of a Christian Heretic* is not what happened to me, but what happened *in* me, my encounters with the ever-expanding consciousness God is. This is my authority for the things I write and say and the life I live. This is not the path of a single man; it is humanity's path.

Each person must experience the First Light. Each must think, speak, and act from the authority of personal spiritual birth and ongoing revelations. This is the foundational message of the founders of all religions and ways of life—personal revelation. It is the authority, and this belief is heresy.

A way of life based on dogma, creeds, and ancient sacred texts is rooted in antiquity. This can be helpful, but it must not supersede the authority of personal experience with God. My way of life requires rebirth, spiritual breakthroughs and revelations, and these encounters may impart insights different from established beliefs, creeds, and dogma. When differences arise, I am told, "Believe, have faith." I reply, "Be still and know, and what is known will inform your faith. Have experiences, and they will become the authority for what you think, say, and do."

I acknowledge and pay homage to the past. It was my beginning, my teacher, and it taught me that all religions begin as individual spiritual experiences. Sacred texts record these events. The authority is not the religion or its scriptural record, but the experience that birthed the religion and etched a recording on stone or papyrus or paper. This means every person is destined to speak with authority, for every person is destined to experience the Ever-Expanding Consciousness.

The Strange Path of Heresy

My spiritual experiences are my authority, and yet what I know today, I may discard tomorrow. This is the strange path of heresy. On the first day, a revelation appears to be heresy. How can trees create the wind? How can my life be God's prayer? Is God really consciousness?

I think these ideas and additional insights appeared in my consciousness for my consideration. I often wrestled with them for years before I accepted the gift and meaning of the words. Every experience, every insight I share with you, I share for your consideration in the hope that you like to wrestle.

Religious leaders want their beliefs to stand forever, but there is only one belief that is true for everyone all the time. The truth of today may become the error of tomorrow.

On whose authority shall I live? The insights of the past? The books of antiquity? Perhaps, but each insight and verse of scripture must be put to the test. My authority comes not from what happened to others, but what happens in me.

Dogma demands belief. This has been humanity's path to truth, dependence on the insights of people of the past. The heretical path puts the insights of the ancients to the test, and it demands spiritual birth today.

When a supposed truth is presented to me, I do not agree or disagree. I test it, draw conclusions and may believe. This is one way to know what is true. There is another—be still and know. This is the way of personal revelation and spiritual breakthrough.

What I have described to you is the swirl of thoughts, beliefs, and insights that live in my mind. There is no arrogance here. There is no declaration of righteousness or correctness. There is no heresy. No one considers his beliefs heretical, but they may be. Only the Spirit of Truth illumines us, and its ways are "put it to the test," and "be still and know."

Heretical Ideas

As I write today, I realize soon I will finish *An Autobiography of a Christian Heretic.* Life is lived, but it must be examined, every challenge dissected and every heretical thought considered. Most of life is not what happens in our outer or inner world, but the wonderings, ponderings, dissections, and reflections on the happenings.

One failed relationship, one disease, one chance encounter with another person, one poor decision, one heretical insight, one spiritual experience, seed thoughts, feelings, images and questions about who we are, why we are, and if there is a God.

Tragic events and their thoughts can radiate darkness, but such events and thoughts can eventually shine light on our life. We can see into the shadows of the difficult times and see we were not alone, that loving arms carried us or that a nearby truth waited to be discovered.

The Heart Event

I encountered such a time. I call it "the heart event." In 2013, before my body had a heart attack… Notice I did not write I had a heart attack. I am not my body. I am consciousness and therefore incapable of having a heart attack, but the body I am currently using has its experiences, and because we are so "close," the event can impact me. As you will soon see, this revelation was my downfall and my deliverance.

Years before my body had a heart attack, I went for a jog and experienced a classic sign of a heart problem, pain radiating down my left arm. I returned home, but did not tell Nancy what happened. I went online and explored the symptom and conveniently concluded there was no heart problem, it was indigestion.

Later additional symptoms arose, dizziness and chest discomfort. Tums seemed to help, supporting my illusion of indigestion. And yet, often I walked and exercised with no discomfort. I was okay, or so I thought.

One Sunday afternoon Nancy and I went for a walk. I made it only to the end of the driveway before the "indigestion" caused me to return home. I sat on the couch and lost consciousness for an instant. On Tuesday, I was at hospice with a dying friend and his family. I felt chest discomfort walking to my car after he made his transition.

The next day, I counseled at the office in the morning, returned home and hit a few golf balls on the range, and after each stroke, I paused because of the pain. The pain quickly subsided, and I hit another ball, and the pain returned. I went home. Nancy could tell something was wrong. A heart event was under way, but it was not the real problem. The real problem was denial.

Nancy called our good friend and church nurse Karen Reed. She told Nancy she would meet us at the emergency room. I said I wasn't going. Karen asked to talk to me. I told Nancy I didn't want to talk to Karen. This belligerent behavior was not like me. It is amazing what fear can do.

That evening Nancy and I went to church, and I prepared for my class, *The Art of Spiritual Healing* based on the book by Joel Goldsmith. An ironic title considering what was about to happen.

As I lit the candles and set up my class materials, the chest pain intensified. I blew out the candles, and told Nancy I needed to go the hospital. She drove me to Healthpark Medical Center. When we arrived, I felt no pain and walked into the emergency room, but I was scared. Karen arrived and I was given an EKG and assigned a room. John Reed, Karen's husband, joined us, and we sat together in the room.

A doctor arrived, sat on the edge of the bed, patted my leg, and told me about the heart attack and that it was still happening. I was admitted to the hospital and Nancy and I stayed overnight awaiting test results and a course of treatment.

The next day, Halloween, I underwent catherization to find and alleviate arterial blockage through the insertion of a stent. As I waited for the procedure, I told the nurse who was dressed as an angel (Not a good visual for someone whose body was in the midst of a heart event) that I was in pain. It was a seven on a scale of ten, with ten being unbearable. I received a pill, and the pain subsided. Doctor Lee did the procedure, and as I regained consciousness, he told me the blockage was too severe for stents. He prescribed a pump to support my heart, and then he told Nancy and two friends, Karen Reed and Carla Palmer, that emergency bypass surgery was required. Three arteries were blocked, one 100% blocked, another 99% blocked and a third 90% restricted. The only reason I was still of the earth was that my body had made small ancillary vessels around the blockage.

Nancy called our sons, Jamie and Ben, and asked them to come. A successful triple bypass was performed the next day. The body's recovery was under way, but what about the real issue?

Getting To Know My Sacred Human

The gift of the kidney donation was a realization of my spiritual nature. Remember, the vision of the vortex of light, the interconnection of all things and the message, "Love makes all this possible." The gift of the heart event was not my spiritual nature; it was a hard look at my human nature, the one I call the sacred human.

My earthly experience nearly ended because of denial, because of my lack of willingness to face my humanity. Long ago I pushed aside the belief I was not enough. Now I pushed aside the fact that my body was telling me it was stressed, and its ability to house my soul was threatened. It couldn't be a heart problem. I ate right (so I thought) and exercised. I knew my spiritual identity. Surely, it could not be, and that denial almost became a prophecy in which my physical existence "could not be."

A revelation of the past was reinforced. A spiritual experience can reveal our spiritual nature or our human nature. It can shine light on the truth of our being or the error at the heart of our beliefs and behavior. The heart event showed me the sacredness of being human. Remember, the sacred human was one of the great discoveries of my life.

A glimpse of the sacredness of being born of water is precious. Who does not smile when a babe is born? Physical birth and spiritual birth create the possibility of balance, so we can be fully human and fully divine and consequently fully alive. As a result of the heart event, I was more honest with myself, more willing to embrace my foibles. I entered more confidently into the darkness of my soul. I went deeper into my humanity not to purge it, but to become aware of it and to accept it, to love myself.

When I was in denial, I was not fully alive. I not only denied pain and unpleasant things; I denied parts of myself, and as a being whose primary nature is consciousness, there is much I could not see.

Through the heart event, a past revelation became real—*unless you are willing to experience your humanity, you won't be able to express your divinity.* The experience of my humanity and my willingness to accept it caused scales to fall from my eyes. I became more aware, more like a child filled with awe, wonder, and curiosity.

The pure consciousness of the First Light is true to Its nature, always on an eternal quest to be more conscious, always exploring, curious and filled with wonder. There is no labeling or judgment. What is encountered is accepted, embraced, and put to the test.

I see this clearly now. To be alive is to be aware and for me the expansion of consciousness comes through living life and through revelation. We are born of water and Spirit, and both births support the nature of being—consciousness.

Ah, Yes or Oh, No

There were life challenges like the heart event and spiritual revelations like "nothing needs to happen." Sometimes life events and revelations took years to unravel, at other times the breakthrough in consciousness was immediate. Growth of consciousness did not stop as I wrote this book. In fact, the idea that God is the Ever-Expanding Consciousness, the First Light, happened in the midst of writing *An Autobiography of a Christian Heretic*. It was a heretical revelation, one that I wanted to dismiss, but it persisted and so did I.

Other revelations made me feel like a child and caused no consternation. Immediately, I knew they were true. My soul said, "Ah, yes." This contented sigh was different from my soul's outburst when the EEC appeared, "Oh, no." However, whether my soul cries, "Ah, yes," or "Oh, no," all revelations are subject to the only enduring truth of a heretic. The truth of today may be the error of tomorrow.

It's All Heresy

Much of religion still trembles at a thought of God. The mysterious, terrible god who lived on the mountain and caused the ground to shake still lives in our collective consciousness. Even though we are told we are made in the image of the Creator, we irrationally cling to the belief that our nature is innately evil.

Conveniently, we formed a belief that our merciful god created hell to keep us on the straight and narrow. Surely fear will raise us up and bring us salvation. This we believe, and it is heresy. The *I am that I am* is forgotten, and our true nature is forsaken.

The terrible god, hell, and our evil nature are examples of heresy becoming the way. We believe, form our creeds and defend the god envisioned by people who lived thousands of years ago. Some seekers plumb these ancient beliefs against personal revelation and daily living. They conclude the truth of yesteryear is the error of today. New insights and understanding are sought. Seekers are born again; their spiritual experiences expand their consciousness and new insights and ideas are entertained. The new "truth" is called heretical, but eventually it becomes the way until there is another spiritual birth.

This is humanity's path, a cosmic circle where heresy is the way. We don't call our beliefs heresy; we call them truth, and we should, but let us always remember, "we are always half-way there;" the journey is infinite. The truth of today will be the error of tomorrow, and so we continuously test and conclude, and we heed the call to "be still and know."

Such Uncertainty

It seems we live in a state of uncertainty. Consciousness is always expanding; discovering the world is round, and new revelations reveal the flatness of our current beliefs. Heresy is the way, for the revered truth of yesteryear is the heresy of today, and the truth of today will become the heresy of tomorrow. We wonder what is true and how shall we live.

We have a choice. We can live in uncertainty and cling to our beliefs, or we can live as children of the Infinite; filled with curiosity and wonder, filled with the desire to become more conscious and heed the call to be the light of the world. We can weave a protective cocoon and become defenders of the faith, or we can weave a chrysalis and emerge as a new species aware of the infinite journey and the quest to awaken again and again.

More provisions for the journey….

1. Heresy is a question of authority.
2. The authority is our personal experience of God.
3. Only the Spirit of Truth illumines us, and its ways are "put it to the test" and "be still and know."
4. Ah, yes or Oh, no.
5. Heresy is the way, for the truth of today will be the error of tomorrow.

Come with me. Only one thing remains to share with you. How does an explorer of the Infinite live—one who is as childlike as its Creator, one who hears and heeds the call to be the light of the world, how does this one live?

CHAPTER TWENTY-TWO

Allegiances

Credo

In the second year of ministerial training, all students took a class entitled, "Credo." Credo is Latin; it means I believe. The professor challenged us and guided us to discover our beliefs about ourselves and God. We explored the human dilemma and asked what ideas and tools were needed to live a life of purpose. The course concluded when we wrote our Credo paper and presented our beliefs to our classmates.

My credo began with the human dilemma. A chick fell out of its nest and was raised by rabbits. The bird believed it was a rabbit. The bunnies hopped from place to place and so did the bird. It was created to fly, but it did not. It sometimes looked up and saw creatures flying from branch to branch and soaring in the sky. The impostor rabbit wondered who these winged creatures might be. The bird felt divine discontent, not because it did not fly, but because it did not know its name, its nature.

This is our dilemma. We believe we are one thing, a creature destined to hop on the ground when we are made to soar. We believe we are flesh and blood when we are expressions of the ever-expanding consciousness God is. We feel anguish because we live a lie and limit our potential.

My credo presentation followed a revolutionary path. I, like Jesus, called God Father. It was a radical idea. Jesus introduced closeness of God to the human family. Prior to this time, God was set apart. In the Jewish tradition, God resided in the Temple in the Holy of Holies. Through experience, Jesus knew He was more than close to God; He was *one* with God. Jesus' prayer was "I and the Father are one."

In my credo presentation, I called God Father and affirmed I was a child of God with a divine inheritance or potential. Fifty years ago, this was my beginning, a sacred seed of conscious oneness with God that bears fruit today.

Now, I write a new credo. The human dilemma is the same—we don't know who or what we are. To know ourselves, we must first know the nature of God. We are made in the image and after the likeness of God, but what is this image?

The Image of God

There are few examples of God naming Itself, but here is one. It was on Mount Horeb. Remember, we were there with Moses, and we heard the Creator reveal Its nature—*I am that I am.* God is pure consciousness, and I am an individualized expression of the consciousness God is. When I became a sentient being, I spoke as an expression of consciousness—I am. This is my new credo. Once I lived as a child of God. It was a good life. Remember, the focus of the first couple of years of my ministry was I and the Father are one. Oneness was the best beginning, but it expanded on Mount Horeb where I learned God is consciousness. Doors opened, scales fell from my eyes, but the age-old question remained.

The Question

How shall I live? If God is consciousness, and I am an expression of this First Light, I have access to all that God is. Everything is known through consciousness—even God. I can live from this awareness. In this way, the EEC has an avenue of expression and another means to gather to Itself awareness and applied truth.

And so, I returned to the life of a shepherd—solitude and stillness, waiting and loving. This, of course, means prayer/meditation and incorporating *be still and know that I am God* into daily practices. Not to conceive prayers as the Celts did when they churned butter or plowed their fields, but to make stillness and silence a part of my daily life. It is to be in the world, but not of it. I call this Allegiance to Silence.

Allegiance to Silence

Ideally, my day begins with a sense of the Presence. Each day I stand on the deck of our mountain cabin and "greet the day." The day might begin with an awareness of God, but the activities of daily living can overshadow the subtlety of perpetual oneness. Obviously, life is best lived maintaining an awareness of the ever-expanding consciousness God is, but the connection is delicate, like the fragrance of a flower in the garden.

It begins with being still, waiting and loving, remembering the fabric of creation is oneness; all things joined one to another. This is essential, but it is not enough. To daily prayer/meditation I added three-day silent retreats when I took with me no books or media, just a steno pad and a pen. I brought my food and spoke to no one during my three days of silence. Remembering and renewal are required to notice the subtle fragrance of the garden, the interconnectedness of all things.

Remembering and Renewal

As a minister in the field, my days were filled with counseling. Hour upon hour, I listened to those I served, and I shared the truth I knew. Each meeting began with five minutes of silence. The more people I counseled with during the day, the more five-minute periods of silence I experienced.

Staff appointments and board meetings began with silence. The periods of silence expanded before classes. Prior to a class, I invited the congregation to join me for 25 minutes of silence. Usually, this was unguided meditation. We simply sat together.

The congregation in Raleigh, North Carolina was remarkable. There was an allegiance to silence in this ministry. We shared many classes together and 30-40 people came before each class to sit in silence. The remarkable thing about this incredible group of seekers was that even when there was no class, they came to sit in stillness for a half-an-hour.

When you give allegiance to silence, minutes are not the segments that join the events of the day. Monastic moments of stillness, sitting, silence, waiting and loving, are the new elements of time.

Before every significant event, before every service, every memorial, every wedding, every radio or television interview, I was still. I tried to live from a consciousness of the First Light.

It is constructive to know when a challenging event lies ahead and to prepare for it by being still, but this is not always possible. Suddenly, great challenges can appear. There is no time to be still or to engage in five minutes of silence. Action is required, and it is required now. An Allegiance to Consciousness makes this possible.

Allegiance to Consciousness

Any state of mind lingers. Something at work unsettles us. We are angry. The stimulus is no more, but anger lingers. We return home, and it is obvious to our loved ones that something is wrong. We all experience this aspect of consciousness lingering.

The good news is that a consciousness of the First Light lingers. This is why we practice the Presence and engage in monastic moments and go apart awhile. It is why I give allegiance to silence, for it gives birth to spiritual consciousness. It led me to an allegiance to consciousness.

The connection with the consciousness God lingers, and we can live from this fragment of a divine encounter. For instance, a person who gives allegiance to silence and consciousness drives through a quiet, residential neighborhood. Children are at play. The driver is naturally cautious, but suddenly has the feeling—stop the car. A ball rolls between two parked automobiles, and a child in pursuit dashes into the road. The little one is unharmed. This is divine consciousness lingering. There is guidance, and it is followed.

This is how I live. I give allegiance to silence and consciousness. I am not alone. I have access to the Ever-Expanding Consciousness, and I am an expression of the First Light. I hear the call to be the light of the world. However, not only do I give allegiance to silence and consciousness; I give Allegiance to Mystery.

Allegiance to Mystery

The most astonishing things that happened in my life were not planned. I did not plan to meet Nancy at her church on the Sunday morning in Norfolk, Virginia when John Bassette gave a sermon in song. Our meeting was a mysterious encounter that changed both our lives. The effects of this meeting in 1968 continue today.

My allegiance to mystery was part of my search to find a balanced life. The Ever-Expanding Consciousness lives in me as curiosity and wonder, and I wondered how I could live a mystical life and fulfill my responsibilities of daily living. I saw the promise: *seek first the kingdom...and all else shall be added unto me.*

There it was. Be true to my nature—consciousness—and seek to become increasingly aware, and the awareness that grows in me will manifest itself as all that is needed for daily living. Later I learned how important it is to continue to give allegiance to the silence to receive ideas and insights to guide my daily life.

I took a hard line when the thought came to me *manifestation is none of my business*, while at the same time knowing manifestation would occur. However, it would not be my purpose. What came into being was added. The allegiance to mystery was reinforced by another thought: *nothing needs to happen.* These strange words brought peace, and I knew they were a bridge from the unseen to the seen, from possibilities to what is possible. "Nothing needs to happen" helped me let go.

As I write, memories come that reveal seeds sprouting and calling me to mystery. Before I was ordained, I tried out at two Georgia churches, both study groups, one in Augusta and another in Athens. I was asked to write an article for the newsletter of the Atlanta church that sponsored the two study groups. My article was called, "Living Beyond Cause and Effect." Here it is again, I am to seek the kingdom, a consciousness of God, and all else will be added unto me. Even in the early months of 1976, the seed was planted. It took decades for the harvest to come and a life of meekness to be lived. Remember, Jesus said the meek inherit the earth. This is a strange saying. Who are the meek, how do they live and what do they know that enables them to inherit the earth?

The meek are powerful because they know the power of consciousness and how it works. Once a consciousness dawns in us, it begins its journey into manifestation. It is mysterious because no one can predict the shape and form of the manifestation, but it will be added.

What comes into being comes through inheritance. We inherit something not because of what we do, but because of what we are, because of our name or nature. This is why the meek are peaceful and non-resistant. Their work is done in silence, in the causative realm of consciousness. Once established, life flows from the ever-expanding consciousness God is. This is why I give allegiance to consciousness.

Allegiances

My life flows from my allegiances. I give Allegiance to Consciousness, to wonder, awe, and curiosity, for I feel the desire to become increasingly aware. I am a child entering the kingdom of God. I give Allegiance to Silence, to being still, to waiting and to loving. I see the kingdom of God is here. I give Allegiance to Mystery, to meekness, for who can know the shape of "added things?" Added things cannot help us live as we are destined to live. We are primarily consciousness, destined to be lights of the world, to be invisible men and women who speak without saying a word—He who has seen me has seen the First Light.

Allegiance to Service

In a dream, I came to a chasm. There was a bridge. I looked ahead. A person on the other side of the chasm waved at me and walked toward me. Without saying a word, the person took my hand and led me across the bridge.

I wondered if we were going to travel together. The person shook his head. "No, you must stay and help another to cross the chasm. You can't go forward until you help another. The bridge is called, 'Two By Two.'"

Just as the animals entered the ark two by two, so each person must extend a helping hand to another. There will always be someone standing at the bridge. And when the last one comes to cross the chasm, all of us will be there to help, for no one is left behind.

How Shall I Live?

This is how I live—the Four Allegiances: Silence, Consciousness, Mystery, and Service. Each allegiance gives rise to another. Silence allowed me to know God's name and nature, "I am that I am"—Pure consciousness. This is the image in which I am made. It is constantly being made manifest, but no one knows its ways. It gives birth to mystery, and faith is born. Finally, it is known that the lights of the world are one. None is free until all are free, so I yield to another allegiance—service.

Until today, I did not know the Four Allegiances; I only knew the First Light was seeking expression in and through and as me. Today as I write the last chapter of *An Autobiography of a Christian Heretic* I see the four allegiances for the first time.

It is said we live life one day at a time, but life is not a matter of days; it is a matter of revelations, spiritual breakthroughs, and spiritual births. May the provisions below nourish you. May they be your daily bread, living water and manna to eat you have never known before. May they give you strength not to say a prayer, but strength to hear and be the prayer that God prays.

My Provisions for the journey...

1. God is consciousness.
2. I am an individualized expression of the ever-expanding consciousness God is.
3. My purpose is to awaken and to be increasingly aware.
4. My practice is waiting and loving.

5. I am committed to the Four Allegiances: Allegiance to Silence, Allegiance to Consciousness, Allegiance to Mystery, and Allegiance to Service.
6. This is how I live.

Won't you join me?

Other Books By Jim Rosemergy

The Watcher
The Gathering
The Third Coming
The Sacred Human
A Recent Revelation
The Transcendent Life
The Quest For Meaning
A Closer Walk With God
The Prayer That God Prays
Living The Mystical Life Today
Even Mystics Have Bills To Pay
A Daily Guide To Spiritual Living
How To Be A Wick In God's Candle
The Seeker, A Boy In Search Of His Name
Attaining The Unattainable, The Will Of God

To email Jim Rosemergy: jimrosemergy@gmail.com
Website: Jimrosemergy.com

Made in United States
North Haven, CT
28 August 2022